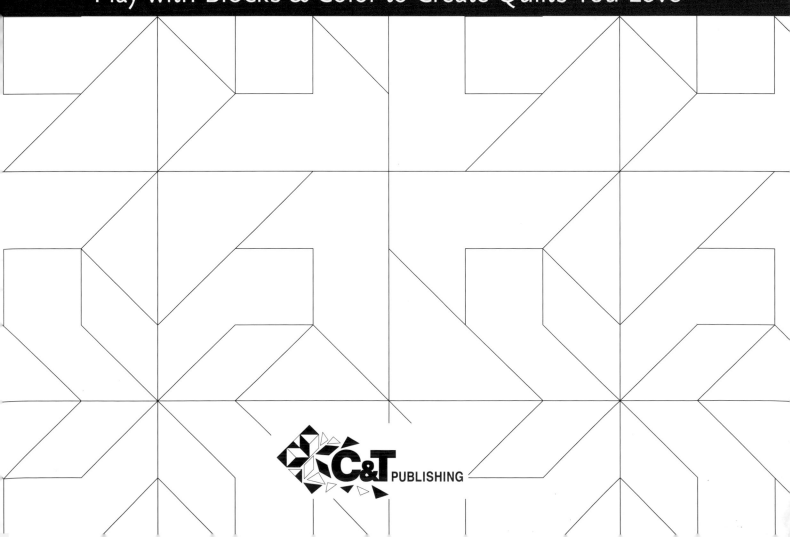

DESIGNING QUILTS IS EASY!

Wayne Kollinger

Play with Blocks & Color to Create Quilts You Love

C&T PUBLISHING

Publisher: Amy Marson

Creative Director: Gailen Runge

Acquisitions Editor: Susanne Woods

Editor: Liz Aneloski

Technical Editors: Sandy Peterson and Amanda Siegfried

Copyeditor/Proofreader: Wordfirm Inc.

Cover/Book Designer: Kristy K. Zacharias

Production Coordinator: Zinnia Heinzmann

Production Editor: Julia Cianci

Illustrator: Aliza Shalit

Photography by Christina Carty-Francis and Diane Pedersen of C&T Publishing, Inc., unless otherwise noted.

Published by C&T Publishing, Inc., P.O. Box 1456, Lafayette, CA 94549

Library of Congress Cataloging-in-Publication Data

Kollinger, Wayne.

 Designing quilts is easy! : play with blocks & color to create quilts you love / Wayne Kollinger.

    p. cm.

  ISBN 978-1-57120-783-8 (softcover)

1. Patchwork--Design. 2. Quilts--Design. I. Title.

 TT835.K643 2010

 746.46'041--dc22

                          2009026799

Printed in China

10 9 8 7 6 5 4 3 2 1

Acknowledgments

I knew my wife, Linda Hurd, was a quilter before I married her. What I didn't know then was that I would become one too, or that I would write a quilt book. I am grateful for her encouragement and input, and for the many quilts she sewed for the book. She endured a good deal of inconvenience while I was writing. I cannot thank her enough; this book could not have happened without her help.

I also want to thank Doreen Folk and Joan Vogel of the Fabric Cottage in Calgary, Alberta, for their support. They critiqued an early version of this book and were the first to suggest I try teaching classes.

Thanks as well to everyone at C&T for helping to make my dream a reality.

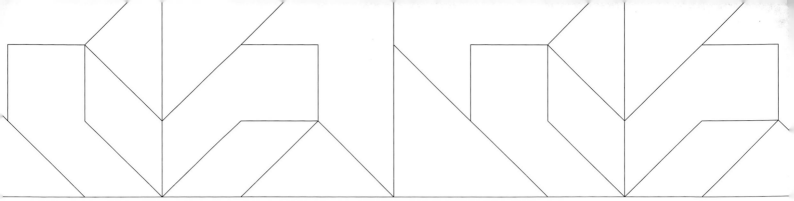

Contents

Introduction

Designing quilts is enjoyable, easy, and addictive. It is less work to design a quilt than to sew one. So why don't more quilters design their own quilts? Maybe it's because no one has ever shown them how. This book shows you an easy way to design your own quilts.

The book is divided into three parts: What If? What Next? and What Else? These are followed by six projects in the Appendix.

Endiang, Wayne Kollinger, 2005, 24½″ × 33½″

PART 1 WHAT IF?

The first part introduces a design process that is based on three simple questions: "What if...?" "Do I like it?" and "Why?" There is nothing new about these three questions; you've asked them all your life. They are the basis of all design.

Part 1 *explains* how to use these questions to design. However, if you've ever tried to learn a new game, you know it takes more than just having the rules explained; you need to see the game played. Learning to design is no different.

Part 1 also *demonstrates* how to use the questions. In it, I design six quilts while you look over my shoulder and eavesdrop on my thoughts. You will watch quilt designs develop step by step. You will see how easy it is to design when you ask, "What if...?" "Do I like it?" and "Why?"

Part 1 ends with a brief review of some of the design principles and design strategies that are used in the demonstrations.

PART 2 WHAT NEXT?

It is very satisfying to look at a quilt design and think, "I designed that." But now you have to sew it. You need to study your design and answer the question, "How am I going to do this?" You need a plan. Part 2 shows you how to create that plan. It shows you how to divide a pattern into sewable sections and how to calculate fabric quantities.

PART 3 WHAT ELSE?

Part 3 expands on the design process introduced in Part 1. To keep things simple while I explained the design process, I focused on quilts with only six blocks. Part 3 goes beyond that and shows you how to explore endless possibilities.

This part also explores how to adapt a design you've created to a variety of different quilts: placemats, table runners, lap quilts, wallhangings, and bed quilts.

Part 3 shows you how to adapt the design process to all kinds of quilt projects. You might want to try designing pieced pictures or even alphabets. Or you might want to appliqué or embroider your quilts. Or you might want to quilt clothing or bags. Once you understand the design process, these are all possible.

APPENDIX

In Part 1, you watched as I designed six quilts. You will find step-by-step instructions for all of those quilts in the Appendix. If you should decide to make them, I would be pleased and flattered. If, however, you would rather keep them for inspiration and instead create your own quilt designs, then I would be so proud of you that people would think I'm your mother.

Athabasca 2, Linda Hurd, 2007, 24½″ × 33½″

PART 1:

WHAT IF?

Every quilter can be a quilt designer.

Quilt design is not some mysterious art to be practiced by a select few. Nor is it particularly difficult to do. In fact, designing a quilt takes less time and effort than sewing one. Like most things, once you know how, it's easy.

As a quilter you already know a lot about design—more than you think you do. You've probably done some design by making small changes to a pattern. Maybe you picked different colors. Or perhaps you changed the border. You might have added some embellishments or had a better idea for the quilting. You didn't think of it as design, but it was.

You made those changes by asking yourself questions. Questions that you didn't even know you asked, because you asked them subconsciously. In Part 1 you are going to learn to ask those questions out loud and use them to do more as a designer.

CHAPTER 1:
Do Something

"Do something—anything—then change it and keep changing it until you like it."

That is often the first thing I tell myself when I start to design a quilt. And it is always what I tell myself when I get stuck.

Any serious writer, artist, composer, or quilter will tell you that waiting for inspiration is a mistake. Creative people don't wait for great ideas before they start; they just start and then the great ideas come.

It's easy to say, "Just start." But where do you start? What do you do?

Start anywhere. Do anything. Pick colors or fabrics. Choose a block or a setting. Doodle on paper (graph paper is great for quilt doodling). Play with patterns or textures or shapes. Audition bits of fabric. It doesn't matter where or how you start. What matters is that you start.

Design is a treasure hunt, a chance to look for hidden ideas. It's not an exercise in problem solving. If you've been thinking of it that way, stop it! You already have enough problems. What you need is adventure. Go hunting for treasure.

Treasure won't come looking for you; you have to go looking for it. But when you do, something wonderful happens. You discover that treasure is everywhere.

For years your subconscious has saved images of sunsets, cities, flowers, seashells, quilts, and winter storms. It has files full of colors, shapes, patterns, and textures. And it has opinions on everything. It is itching to share all this with you. Start designing, and before long it's at your elbow saying, "Why don't you do this? Why not try that?" You will have more than enough ideas to keep you going.

A design philosophy such as "Do something, then change it until you like it" is useless without some means of putting it into practice. You need a design process. The next chapter introduces a design process that consists of asking, and then answering, three very simple questions.

Rosebud, Linda Hurd, 2006, 24½" × 33½"

CHAPTER 2:
Three Questions

Linden/Squares, Wayne Kollinger, 2007, 24½" × 33½"

There are three questions that are key to design. They are: **"What if...?"** **"Do I like it?"** and **"Why?"** Half of design time is spent asking these three questions over and over again, and the other half is spent answering them.

The design process ends when, instead of asking these questions, you find yourself admiring your design and asking, "When can I sew this quilt?"

There is nothing remarkable about these three questions. People ask them all the time. At any quilt show you'll hear: "This would be nice in pink and mauve." (This is the result of asking, *"What if* I change the colors?") "Marge, you've got to see this; it is gorgeous!" (The result of asking, *"Do I like it?"*) "That's not for me. It's too busy." (The result of asking, *"Why* don't I like it?")

People are not aware that they ask these questions, nor of how often they ask them. But these questions are essential to the design process.

Let's look at each of these three questions.

1. WHAT IF...?

The first question is: "What if...?" Its purpose is to evoke a creative response. It asks for something new, different, or innovative.

"What if...?" is open ended. It has a blank space for you to fill in. It asks you to go and hunt among your memories for something to fill that blank. You can fill that blank with anything. It can be something simple and obvious. Or it can be something complex and obscure. The choice is yours.

Suppose you want to choose colors. You begin by asking, "What if...?" "What if I try autumn colors?" "What if I use analogous colors?" "What if I pick colors at random?"

Keep in mind that your initial choices are not necessarily your final choices. During the design process you will be questioning your choices.

Suppose you start with a palette of autumn colors—red, orange, gold, and yellow. As you design, you might ask, "What if the red were darker?" "What if the orange had more yellow in it?" "What if I use brown instead of gold?" "What if I include some green?" You might even ask, "What if I switch to candy colors?" Asking, "What if...?" is an easy way to go exploring.

Cochrane/West Valley, Wayne Kollinger, 2006, 24½" × 33½"

2. DO I LIKE IT?

The second question is: "Do I like it?" Its purpose is to evoke an aesthetic response. It asks for an emotional reaction. It asks for an opinion.

Suppose you asked, "What if I try a darker red?" Now you have to decide, "Do I like it?" "Does this appeal to me?" "Is this what I want?" This question is all about you. What do you like? What do you want? This should be an easy question to answer because you are the expert on you.

You are also an expert at asking, "Do I like it?" because you ask it constantly. Whenever you read a book, watch a movie, go shopping, or do anything, you ask yourself, "Do I like it?" Most of the time, you're not aware that you asked yourself a question. You are so good at it that it has become automatic and subconscious. For a time, while you are learning to design, you will need to ask, "Do I like it?" out loud.

The answer to "Do I like it?" is not always yes or no. A range of answers is possible: "I hate it," "I've seen worse," "I don't know," "I've seen better," "Maybe," "It's okay," "I absolutely love it." The list goes on and on. There are many degrees of liking. When you are designing, you will need to decide just how much you like, or dislike, the things you try.

Of the three questions, this is the one that determines when a design is finished. If something is only okay, then you still need to improve it. If you've found something you absolutely love, then you're done.

Sometimes you don't know if you like something until you compare it to something else. Then the answer is: "I like this better than that." This is a very useful answer. It gives you direction.

You are undecided about a design you've created. At random, you replace a red with a darker red. Then you compare the two designs. If you like the darker red better, you may want to try an even darker one. If you like it less, you may want to try a lighter one. Or, you may decide that changing the red is not the answer and try something else.

Remember, "Do I like it?" is a very personal question. Not everyone likes the same things. You will discover that you have your own aesthetic, your own style. You will also discover that your aesthetic and your style change as you grow as a designer.

Lowland Heights, Wayne Kollinger, 2008,
24½″ × 33½″

3. WHY?

The third question is: "Why?" Its purpose is to evoke an analytical response. It asks you to do some thinking.

You need to know why you like something, or why you don't. You need to know what is working and what isn't. Knowing enables you to make better decisions about what to do next.

A design you created isn't working. You ask why and decide there's too much red in it—way too much red. The next step is obvious: reduce the amount of red. But how? By asking, "What if…?" "What if I replace half the red with purple?" "What if I get rid of the red entirely?" "What if I keep the red in the center of the quilt and replace it with black around the edges?"

"Why?" makes "What if…?" easier by providing a focus.

You don't always know why you like, or don't like, something. Earlier, the problem was not knowing *whether* you liked something; now the problem is not knowing *why* you like something. The solution in both cases is the same: Skip to "What if…?" and make a random change, then compare the two designs. If you like the new design better, or less, the change you made is why.

Sometimes when you ask, "Why?" you get more than one answer. That's good. You now have more than one possibility to explore, more than one "What if…?" you can ask.

One nice thing about asking "Why?" is that you end up teaching yourself design principles. Design principles are just general rules about what is and isn't attractive. By asking, "Why?" you are constantly thinking about the reason that something is or isn't attractive.

Most of the principles you discover this way will be traditional ones, because we all share a common aesthetic. Some of them will be very personal, because you are unique. In either case, the things you learn will help you design your quilts your way.

GOING IN CIRCLES

By now you have a pretty good idea of how the design process works. First, you ask, "What if…?" and try something. Second, you ask, "Do I like it?" Third, you ask, "Why?" for clues about what to try next. Then you ask, "What if…?" and start the cycle again. Eventually, when you ask, "Do I like it?" the answer will be "You bet I do!" At that point you stop designing and start sewing.

In short: Do something—anything—then change it and keep changing it until you like it.

CHAPTER 3:
A Design Game

So far, I've been telling you about the design process. To better understand it, you need to see it in action.

I'm going to design six different quilts in this book. I'll go through the process step by step and tell you what I'm thinking every step of the way. After six quilts, you should have a good grasp of the process and be ready to design on your own.

The design process works with any quilt, but for demonstration purposes I've decided to use Nine-Patch Pinwheel quilts. Although they may not always look like it, these are simple quilts—easy to sew and easy to design.

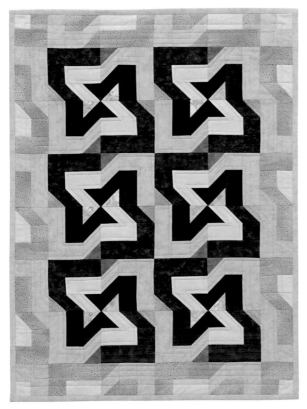

Campsie, Wayne Kollinger, 2008, 24½" × 33½"

WHAT IS A NINE-PATCH PINWHEEL QUILT?

No doubt you have already leafed through the book and looked at the quilts. If I could read minds, I would probably discover that you are wondering, "Why does he call them Nine-Patch Pinwheel quilts? I haven't seen a Nine-Patch block anywhere, and not many pinwheels either. What gives?" Since you asked, I'll tell you.

Look at any collection of quilt blocks and you will discover a large variety of blocks listed as Nine-Patch blocks. As you might expect, you will find Nine-Patch, Nine-Patch variation, and Double Nine-Patch blocks. But you will also find Spool, Calico Puzzle, Shoo Fly, and many others that you don't usually think of as Nine-Patch blocks.

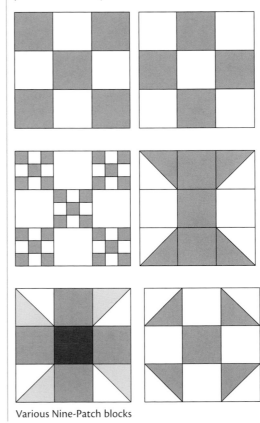

Various Nine-Patch blocks

All of these blocks are designed on a 3 × 3 grid of nine squares and so are called Nine-Patch blocks. They are made by sewing together nine squares of fabric to form a square block. The different block patterns are the result of how the squares are constructed and colored.

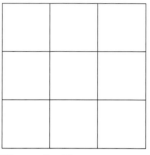

Nine-patch grid

I design a Nine-Patch Pinwheel quilt by first designing a Nine-Patch block.

The Nine-Patch blocks below are typical of the ones I use in my quilt designs. They are not meant to stand alone, but are used as part of a larger block. Because of this, they are not true finished blocks, so I will refer to them as "nine-patch units" from now on.

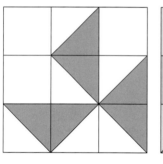
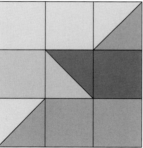

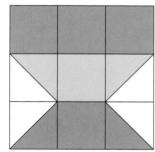
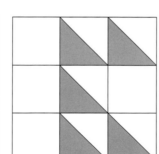

Nine-patch units

That explains the "nine-patch" part of the name. What about the "pinwheel" half?

I remember blowing on pinwheels as a child and watching them spin. Spinning is what pinwheels are all about. It's what they do best.

So what spins in a Nine-Patch Pinwheel block? It's the nine-patch unit. Four copies of a nine-patch unit rotated and joined together make a Nine-Patch Pinwheel block. In effect, the nine-patch units spin around the center point of the Nine-Patch Pinwheel block.

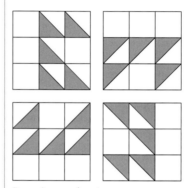

Four nine-patch units

In the example below, it's easy to see a pinwheel. In many of my quilts it's not. But that's part of the fun—disguising the pinwheels and then trying to find them. Now when you leaf through the book, you can look for the Nine-Patch Pinwheel blocks in the quilts.

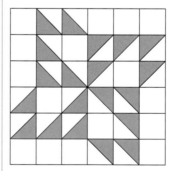

Nine-Patch Pinwheel block

THE NINE-PATCH PINWHEEL GAME

Design is a game. One day, while designing Nine-Patch Pinwheel quilts, I had an "aha" moment—a sudden flash of insight. I realized that I was playing a game. The goal of the game was to design an original Nine-Patch Pinwheel quilt. The rules were very simple, so it was no wonder I enjoyed designing these quilts.

It also occurred to me that if I wrote down the Nine-Patch Pinwheel rules, others could learn them and enjoy the game too. I would be delighted if you were to play the game and design Nine-Patch Pinwheel quilts.

Rule #1 (Nine-Patch Grid)

Designs start on a nine-patch grid with a mandatory half-square triangle whose diagonal runs into a corner.

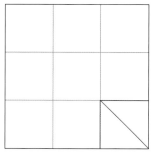

Nine-patch grid with half-square triangle

Rule #2 (Nine-Patch Unit)

Nine-patch units are designed using squares and half-square triangles. These can be placed anywhere in the grid and arranged in any way (except as noted in Rule #1).

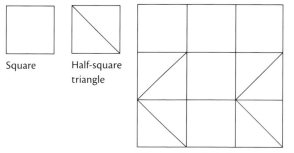

Square   Half-square triangle

Nine-patch-unit design

Rule #3 (Seams)

Unnecessary seams can be eliminated. There is no point in doing more sewing than you have to. (Unless you want to. In which case this rule is optional.)

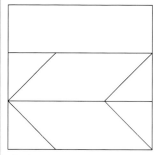

Eliminate unnecessary seams.

Rule #4 (Pinwheel Blocks)

Four nine-patch units are arranged, with their mandatory half-square triangles touching in the center of the block, to make a Nine-Patch Pinwheel block.

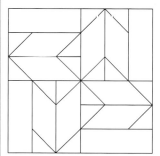

Four nine-patch units make a Nine-Patch Pinwheel block.

Rule #5 (Pinwheel Colors)

Color the nine-patch units (that make up a block) any way you like. They can all be colored the same, or they can all be different.

 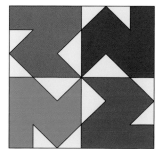

Same colors   Different colors

Rule #6 (Quilt)

Six Nine-Patch Pinwheel blocks with a border make a Nine-Patch Pinwheel quilt.

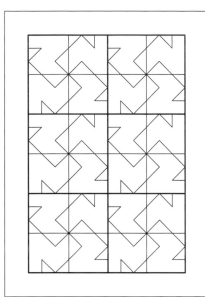

Nine-Patch Pinwheel quilt

There are no rules for borders. You can do anything you want, including nothing at all.

Rule #7 (Quilt Colors)

Color the Nine-Patch Pinwheel blocks any way you like. They can all be colored the same, or they can all be different.

 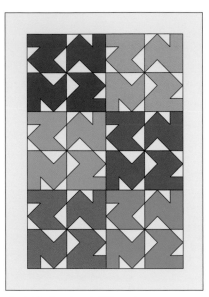

Each block colored the same   Each block colored differently

Rule #8 (The Three R's)

Nine-Patch Pinwheel blocks can be repeated, reflected, or rotated.

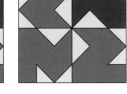

Blocks repeated

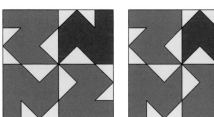

Blocks reflected around a vertical or horizontal line

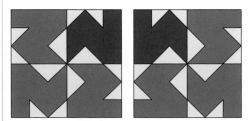

Blocks rotated

WORKSHEET

In order to play the Nine-Patch Pinwheel game, you need to doodle; you need to play with the units, blocks, and quilts. The worksheet below is set up to help you do this.

The easiest way to play (design) these days is on the computer, and you may want to do that. I've created copies of the worksheet on my computer. I design on them using Paint (a general drawing program). When the design is set,

I use EQ6, a quilt designing software program, to make global color changes and test fabric choices.

If you don't have a computer, you can make hard copies of this worksheet, or you could draw on sheets of graph paper.

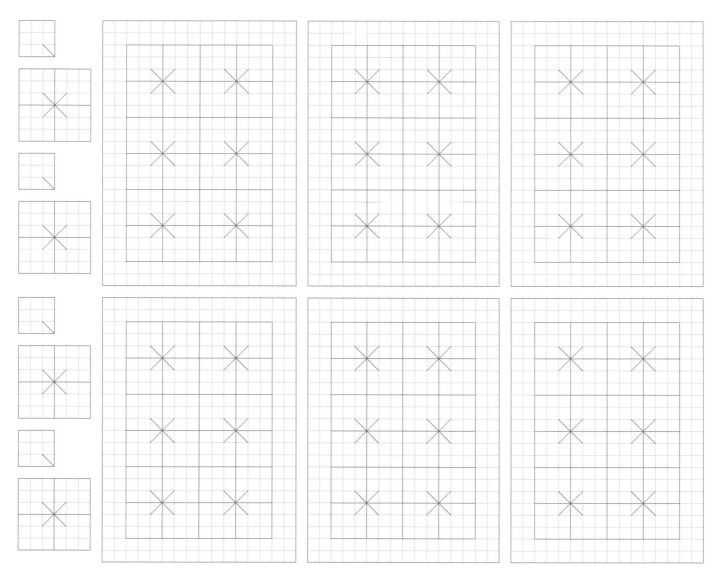

Worksheet

PLAYING THE GAME

1. Start the game by asking, "What if...?" and create a nine-patch unit using squares and half-square triangles. Use that unit 4 times to make a Nine-Patch Pinwheel block. Then use the pinwheel block 6 times to make a quilt.

2. Ask, "Do I like it?"

3. Ask, "Why?"

4. Then ask, "What if...?" and make changes to the blocks and the quilt.

5. Repeat Steps 2–4 as many times as it takes to find a design you want to sew. When you do, the game ends.

Ponoka/School's Out, Linda Hurd, 2006, 42½″ × 33½″

THOUGHTS ON PLAYING THE GAME

To prepare you, I would like to first share a few general thoughts on design for you to keep in mind while you are reading.

Practice Makes Perfect

At first it may seem a bit awkward to ask, "What if...?" "Do I like it?" and "Why?" Anything new is awkward. Learning to drive was awkward. So was learning to sew. But with time new skills become automatic. The design process is just another skill. It will become automatic and you will no longer need to ask the questions out loud. You will ask them without thinking about it, without even knowing that you asked them. However, for now it is important to ask them every time.

Design Is a Voyage

Design is a voyage that often takes you far from where you start—the final design is seldom anything like the initial one. Don't get discouraged if you don't like your first attempts. I seldom do. But I have learned that if I keep making changes I will eventually surprise myself with a quilt I want to sew.

Try Lots of Things

Sometimes a design comes together so quickly that I feel like it's over too soon. I want to keep designing—to keep making changes. So I do. It's always okay to try one more thing, and then another, and another. The final design isn't always the last one you do; it's the one you like best.

Accept Surprises

Sometimes design proceeds in an orderly fashion. One thing leads to the next. Each new idea sparks yet another idea, and there is an obvious progression of thought. But not always. Sometimes a new idea can come out of nowhere, with little relationship to what came before.

That's okay. Inspiration does not have to follow a logical sequence. The important thing is to be able to recognize an opportunity no matter how it arrives.

Change Is Good

You will notice that I sometimes change my mind as I am designing. What I like at first, I don't like later on. What I don't like for one quilt, I do like for a different one. That's because I'm human and because design is a tentative process. It's about trying things and about changing things. There are no set formulas when you design, no absolute right and wrong way to do things. The rules can keep changing as the design changes and as the designer's point of view changes.

That is, until the very end. Eventually you design something you don't want to change, something that you want to have and enjoy. That's when you stop designing, pick fabric, and start sewing.

Take Chances

Designing is about taking chances. To get something new you have to try something different. I sometimes try to create an ugly block to start with. By starting with something odd or crazy, I hope to get out of a rut and do something unique and exciting. Besides, the worse something is, the easier it is to change and improve it.

For *Duchess* (page 37), I use a Nine-Patch Pinwheel block that I don't like to create a quilt I love. Now there's a paradox!

Don't Forget Borders

When you are designing, don't neglect borders. They are fun to experiment with. The goal is to find a border that suits the design. It is always tempting to use a plain border and be done with it. But if you want to display your design to its best advantage, you need to take the time to audition several borders and choose the most appropriate one.

In the case of *Mirror* (page 31), a simple plain border is all that is needed to frame the design. It gives limits to what could otherwise be an endless pattern. In the case of *Duchess* (page 37), no border is needed. The design is complete and requires only a background to rest on. In the case of *Tawatinaw* (page 34), the design is completed in the border. A framing border is added to give more interest to the design.

Rome Wasn't Built in a Day

In Greek mythology, everything King Midas touched turned to gold. The rest of us are not that lucky. All six demonstrations in this book result in quilt patterns. That doesn't always happen. Not every attempt to design a quilt results in a quilt.

When a design I've been trying isn't working and I've run out of ideas, I stop and start a new design. I will return to my stalled design later and try again. I never, never throw anything out. Every quilter that I know has UFOs (unfinished objects); similarly, every quilt designer has UFDs (unfinished designs). Tomorrow, or next week, or several months from now, I will look at a UFD and realize there is still something else I can try. The result is that an ugly duckling often becomes a beautiful swan, and I get another quilt to sew.

Design Is Personal

The language of design can be very personal. As you go through these demonstrations and listen to me talking to myself, you may not always be entirely sure what I mean when I say that something is static, or that it has depth or movement. That's okay. When you start to design you will find that you will begin to develop your own design language.

For now, what is important is learning how the design process works in practice, and realizing that it does work and that it can work for you.

You Can Design

You and I are different. We like different things. We often see things differently. In these demonstration chapters, you might like something I don't. You might see something I don't—something I've overlooked. You might think of something to try that I didn't. That's great! You're starting to think like a designer. Soon you'll be elbowing me to one side and designing on your own.

CHAPTER 4:
Design
Demonstrations

ORION

Wayne Kollinger, 2007, 24½″ × 33½″

I can't imagine trying to learn a game like chess or bridge by just reading the rules. Even a simple game like checkers is easier to learn if someone shows you how to play.

In this chapter, I will play the Nine-Patch Pinwheel game while you look over my shoulder and eavesdrop on my thoughts. I want to show you how easy it is to design a quilt when you repeatedly ask three simple questions: "What if...?" "Do I like it?" and "Why?"

ATTEMPT 1

WHAT IF I start with this simple nine-patch unit? Four of the units rotated make the Nine-Patch Pinwheel block shown below. Six of the blocks repeated make the quilt.

Original unit

Original block

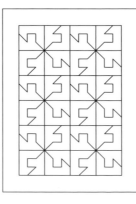

Quilt; blocks repeated

DO I LIKE IT? Not yet.

WHY? It's too plain for me, too regular, and too static.

ATTEMPT 2

WHAT IF I flip some of the Nine-Patch Pinwheel blocks horizontally so that they are mirror imaged?

Original block   New mirror-imaged block

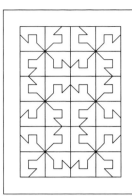

Quilt; original and mirror-imaged blocks

DO I LIKE IT? It's an improvement, but it's still not my cup of tea.

WHY? The shapes don't appeal to me. On some other day, this might spark some ideas, but today I'm not inspired by it.

ATTEMPT 3

WHAT IF I return to Attempt 1 and add another diagonal seam to the original nine-patch unit?

Original unit

New unit with diagonal seam added

New block

Quilt; blocks repeated

DO I LIKE IT? This appeals to me.

WHY? This has more character and more movement. It's starting to look like something. I feel that I might be able to do something with the shapes I see developing.

ATTEMPT 4

WHAT IF I arbitrarily color my pattern using greens and browns?

Block   Colored block

Quilt; blocks repeated

DO I LIKE IT? Not entirely.

WHY? The secondary pattern—two light green pinwheels in the center of the quilt—interests me. However, I find the basic arrangement of two vertical brown columns static.

ATTEMPT 5

WHAT IF I try rotating three of the pinwheel blocks and alternating them with straight blocks? Then some of the brown shapes will be horizontal.

Colored straight block

Rotated block

Quilt; straight and rotated blocks

DO I LIKE IT? A little bit.

WHY? Now that the brown columns are gone, the quilt has more movement. But it needs to be more colorful.

ATTEMPT 6

WHAT IF I selectively replace some of the light green with orange while continuing to use a rotated block arrangement for the quilt?

Block with new color

Rotated block with new color

Quilt; straight and rotated blocks

DO I LIKE IT? Not as much as I did before.

WHY? The orange doesn't add anything. It just breaks up the secondary pattern, creates confusion, and makes the quilt look messy.

ATTEMPT 7

WHAT IF I forget about the orange and add another diagonal seam to the unit? This would create additional shapes and allow me to add more color.

Unit

New unit with diagonal seam added

New block

Quilt; blocks repeated

DO I LIKE IT? Maybe. I don't know yet.

WHY? I need to see how this works when I put the color back in.

ATTEMPT 8

WHAT IF I return to the color scheme in Attempt 5 and add a darker green and a darker brown in the new spaces?

Block with new colors in new areas

Rotated block with new colors in new areas

Quilt; straight and rotated blocks

DO I LIKE IT? This is a slight improvement.

WHY? There is a small pinwheel at the center of the large one, and that creates a little more visual interest. I would like to give more emphasis to the two light green pinwheels in the center of the quilt.

ATTEMPT 9

WHAT IF I replace the light green with white?

Block with new color

Rotated block with new color

Quilt; straight and rotated blocks

DO I LIKE IT? Yes.

WHY? There is more contrast. Now the large pinwheels stand out from the background. The negative white pinwheels in the center of the quilt are more obvious.

ATTEMPT 10

WHAT IF I change the color scheme? Then I can compare and see which colors I like better. What if I try purple and magenta?

Block with new color scheme

Rotated block with new color scheme

Quilt; straight and rotated blocks

DO I LIKE IT? I do. Do I like it better? Yes.

WHY? The purple and magenta are closer in color than the green and brown; this ties each pinwheel together and gives it greater unity. However, I'm not happy yet; I would like it to be more detailed.

ATTEMPT 11

WHAT IF I add yet another diagonal seam? This gives me a new Nine-Patch Pinwheel block and a new quilt pattern using six repeated blocks.

Unit

New unit with diagonal seam added

New block

Quilt; blocks repeated

DO I LIKE IT? Definitely.

WHY? This is very different from what preceded it; it is more interesting. I see all kinds of possibilities in this quilt.

ATTEMPT 12

WHAT IF I color it using an expanded purple and magenta palette?

Block with new colors

Rotated block with new colors

DO I LIKE IT? I am beginning to.

WHY? This has more variety than earlier attempts, in terms of both color and shapes. It is also starting to exhibit some visual texture.

Quilt; straight and rotated blocks

ATTEMPT 13

WHAT IF I switch the colors in some areas? I can move the white from the corners and place it in the centers. I can move the pinks from the pinwheels and place them out in the corners. This creates a series of white pinwheels in the foreground.

Block with switched colors

Rotated block with switched colors

Quilt; straight and rotated blocks

DO I LIKE IT? I don't know.

WHY? The white pinwheels in the foreground are very plain. The background is more developed than the foreground, but there is some interesting movement in the background.

ATTEMPT 14

WHAT IF I replace the white with a new purple?

Block with new color

Rotated block with new color

Quilt; straight and rotated blocks

DO I LIKE IT? Somewhat.

WHY? The quilt finally has a true border. The colors seem richer than they did with the white. But the layout is still too static.

ATTEMPT 15

WHAT IF I replace the very light magenta with a dark red?

Block with new color

Rotated block with new color

Quilt; straight and rotated blocks

DO I LIKE IT? Yes.

WHY? The magentas and reds are close in tone and so they tie together, giving the background greater unity and creating an overall shape. However, the foreground is still static.

ATTEMPT 16

WHAT IF I add a second color to the foreground pinwheel to break it up and de-emphasize it?

Block with new color

Rotated block with new color

Quilt; straight and rotated blocks

DO I LIKE IT? Yes, a little.

WHY? The background figure, which I find more interesting, is starting to take over. The border, which I liked a moment ago, now feels too confining to me.

ATTEMPT 17

WHAT IF I lighten the border and make it part of the light magenta background?

Quilt; new border color, straight and rotated blocks

DO I LIKE IT? Yes.

WHY? I find that the large overall shape that is emerging is interesting; it has some personality.

ATTEMPT 18

WHAT IF I replace the light magenta with white?

Block with new
color

Rotated block
with new color

Quilt; new border color,
straight and rotated blocks

DO I LIKE IT? It's getting better all
the time.

WHY? The increased contrast, both
in tone and color, gives more defini-
tion to the overall shape.

ATTEMPT 19

WHAT IF I replace the light magenta in the pinwheel with white? This has the effect of punching
holes in the image.

Block with new
color

Rotated block
with new color

Quilt; straight and rotated blocks

DO I LIKE IT? Very much.

WHY? The image is now less pon-
derous, less heavy. It has acquired
some delicacy and more interest.

ATTEMPT 20

WHAT IF I make the purple in the pinwheel less
purple and a little closer to magenta?

Block with new
color

Rotated block
with new color

DO I LIKE IT? Yes!

WHY? The new color integrates
better with the rest of the image; in
retrospect the purple looked out of
place.

Quilt; straight and rotated blocks

ATTEMPT 21

WHAT IF I replace the dark red in the
corners with black?

Block with new
color

Rotated block
with new color

Quilt; straight and rotated blocks

DO I LIKE IT? This is it! This is a quilt I want to
make! I'm done.

WHY? The black adds another color, contrast,
depth, and greater variety. The various parts have
separate identities, but they unite to form a cohesive whole. I like the way the negative and positive
shapes work together to move the eye in and
around the image. This quilt is unique, it has character, and it has punch. I enjoy looking at it.

TEES

Wayne Kollinger, 2008, 24½″ × 33½″

ATTEMPT 1

WHAT IF, for my nine-patch unit, I put a triangle inside a rectangle on an angle? Four of the units rotated make the Nine-Patch Pinwheel block. Six of the blocks repeated make the quilt.

Original unit

Original block

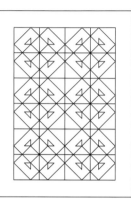

DO I LIKE IT? I do.

WHY? I see latticework that I like and some nice detail.

Quilt; block repeated

ATTEMPT 2

WHAT IF I try a variety of colors?

Block with colors

Quilt; block repeated

DO I LIKE IT? A little.

WHY? The latticework and the fine detail are there, but the background is bland. It needs to be more interesting.

ATTEMPT 3

WHAT IF I create one block with a background of white and light brown, while its center is white and another brown? I can then reverse the browns in a second block. By alternating the blocks, I can create a checkerboard.

Block with new colors

Second block with new colors

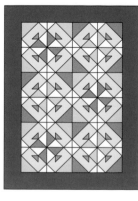

Quilt; blocks alternated

DO I LIKE IT? This is better.

WHY? The background and the border now have separate identities. But the olive yellow rectangles are too much alike; I would like to see more variety.

ATTEMPT 4

WHAT IF I play with how the blocks are colored by adding new colors to the rectangles? And WHAT IF I change the small green triangles to white for more contrast? And WHAT IF I rotate some blocks to create a secondary pattern in the quilt center?

Block with new colors

Second block with new colors

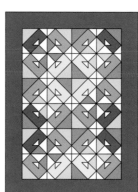

Quilt; rotated blocks

DO I LIKE IT? Oops.

WHY? Now there's too much variety. The olive yellow latticework has disappeared, and the quilt no longer has any apparent structure. However, the olive green is an improvement over the olive yellow; it goes better with the burnt orange.

ATTEMPT 5

WHAT IF I keep the checkerboard background and then feature the burnt orange in one block and the olive green in another?

Block with new color

Second block with new color

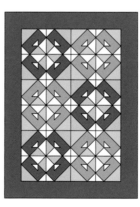

Quilt; alternated blocks

DO I LIKE IT? It's better.

WHY? There's less confusion.

ATTEMPT 6

WHAT IF I try to strengthen the checkerboard effect by replacing the background browns with a light burnt orange in one block and a light green olive in the other?

Block with new colors

Second block with new colors

DO I LIKE IT? Not yet.

WHY? The border bothers me; there's too much orange. The border should not be orange or green. There's too much white as well; it's competing with the dominant shapes.

Quilt; alternated blocks

ATTEMPT 7

WHAT IF I add brown to the triangles at the edge of the blocks? I can use the same brown in the border.

Block with new color

Block with new color

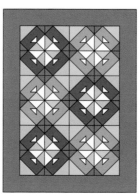

Quilt; new border color, alternated blocks

DO I LIKE IT? I do. I do.

WHY? The brown diamonds formed where the blocks meet are miracle workers. They've brought back the latticework that I liked and that had disappeared while my attention was elsewhere. And they tie the image to the border. However, I'm not totally satisfied yet; the white pinwheels seem a bit weak.

ATTEMPT 8

WHAT IF I replace the white with black?

Block with
new color

Second block
with new color

Quilt; alternated blocks

DO I LIKE IT? Definitely. I want to sew this.

WHY? The black is more impressive than the white. It comes forward, whereas the white recedes. The black also makes the other colors stronger and richer.

ATTEMPT 9

Can I make it even better?

WHAT IF I replace the black with a dark red?

Block with new
color

Second block
with new color

Quilt; alternated blocks

DO I LIKE IT? Not as much.

WHY? The red is okay. It's better than the white but not as commanding as the black.

ATTEMPT 10

A little black did wonders.

WHAT IF I add more and make the border black?

Quilt; new border color

DO I LIKE IT? Not really.

WHY? There's too much black. It's distracting, as it calls too much attention to the border. Attempt 8 works; that's the one I'm going to sew.

Tees Too, Wayne Kollinger, 2007, 24½″ × 33½″

Sometimes fabric choices can affect a design. After I designed *Tees*, I discovered that the colors I wanted were not in my fabric stash (formerly my wife, Linda's, stash, now our stash). So I picked greens, oranges, and browns that were in the stash. The result was that the design changed. But I still like it. I learned that the design process isn't over until the fabric is picked and the quilt has been sewn.

I bought fabrics and made the original *Tees* (page 68). When people ask why there are two versions, I tell them it is to demonstrate the power of color to change a pattern. They don't need to know it was an accident.

LAC DES ARCS

Wayne Kollinger, 2007, 24½" × 33½"

ATTEMPT 1

WHAT IF I try this for my nine-patch unit? Four of the units rotated make the Nine-Patch Pinwheel block. Six of the blocks repeated make the quilt.

Original unit

Original block

DO I LIKE IT? It's not for me.

WHY? There's lots of structure but not much is happening.

Quilt; block repeated

ATTEMPT 2

WHAT IF I do some major renovating by adding four new seamlines?

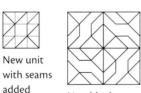

Original unit

New unit with seams added

New block

DO I LIKE IT? This is much better.

WHY? I see movement. This reminds me of a bait can full of wriggling worms.

Quilt; block repeated

ATTEMPT 3

WHAT IF I use two brown tones and create an S-shaped ribbon in the Nine-Patch Pinwheel block? I've ignored the outline pattern in a couple of places. But so what? I can change anything, anytime.

Block with colors

DO I LIKE IT? I like it, but I want to change it.

WHY? There are some interesting shapes in this. I like the diagonal pattern, but I find it a little too repetitive.

Quilt; block repeated

ATTEMPT 4

WHAT IF I alternate 3 straight and 3 rotated blocks?

Block

Rotated block

Quilt; straight and rotated blocks

DO I LIKE IT? This is a definite improvement.

WHY? There is still some structure, but it is less rigid. There is more happening; there is more movement.

ATTEMPT 5

WHAT IF I color the ribbon red to accentuate the pattern?

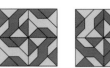

Block with new color

Rotated block with new color

Quilt; straight and rotated blocks

DO I LIKE IT? Another improvement.

WHY? The red is in the foreground and the browns are in the background, so now the quilt has some depth. The movement is still there in both the foreground and the background.

ATTEMPT 6

WHAT IF I add another color and form a second ribbon?

Block with new color

Rotated block with new color

Quilt; straight and rotated blocks

DO I LIKE IT? "Like" is too strong a word. I see potential.

WHY? The caramel brown creates another level of interest. It provides something more to keep my eye occupied. The red and caramel are competing for my attention, so they create some tension and excitement. However, this creates some doubt; is the quilt about the red image or the caramel one?

ATTEMPT 7

WHAT IF I extend the red ribbon—make it longer?

Block with
new color

Rotated block
with new color

DO I LIKE IT? This is a little better.

WHY? The red ribbon is now longer than the caramel one and thus more important. The tension is still there, but the doubt has gone. I also like the fact that the red ribbon now has fewer loose ends.

Quilt; straight and rotated blocks

ATTEMPT 8

WHAT IF I change the red to a series of reds? The ribbon is now light at the center of the pinwheel and dark at the ends of the S shape.

Block with
new colors

Rotated block
with new colors

DO I LIKE IT? Yes.

WHY? This is much brighter—much livelier.

Quilt; straight and rotated blocks

ATTEMPT 9

WHAT IF I try the same trick with the caramel by adding two lighter shades?

Block with
new colors

Rotated block
with new colors

DO I LIKE IT? Yes.

WHY? Again, this is brighter and livelier. The color progression draws the eye along the ribbons and creates visual movement.

Quilt; straight and rotated blocks

ATTEMPT 10

WHAT IF I reduce the contrast in the background browns by changing the dark brown to a lighter shade?

Block with
new color

Rotated block
with new color

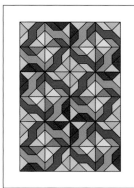

DO I LIKE IT? This is a definite improvement.

WHY? The background was too intrusive. It was interfering with the foreground images. Now it is background again, and the focus is only on the interplay of the red and caramel ribbons.

Quilt; straight and rotated blocks

ATTEMPT 11

WHAT IF I try a red border?

DO I LIKE IT? Nope.

WHY? Too much red. It's distracting.

Quilt; new border color, straight and rotated blocks

ATTEMPT 12

WHAT IF I color the border to match the light brown in the background?

DO I LIKE IT? Much better.

WHY? The focus is on the ribbons, not on the border.

Quilt; new border color, straight and rotated blocks

ATTEMPT 13

WHAT IF I lighten the darkest red?

Block with new color Rotated block with new color

DO I LIKE IT? I do.

WHY? The dark red was too dark; this separated it from the rest of the ribbon. Now the ribbon is a unified whole. It is also just a little brighter.

Quilt; straight and rotated blocks

ATTEMPT 14

WHAT IF I tone down the three shades of caramel?

Block with new color Rotated block with new color

DO I LIKE IT? Yes, indeed. I've found another quilt I can sew.

WHY? I had thought that the caramel added interest by creating tension. Instead it was just creating confusion. Now the red ribbon stands out clearly and the caramel adds interest to the background. I like the various shapes the ribbon makes.

Quilt; straight and rotated blocks

MIRROR

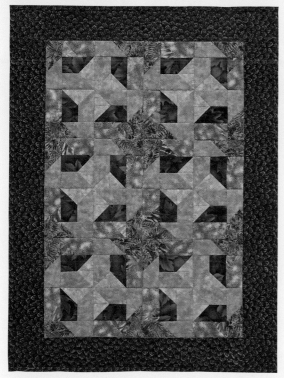

Wayne Kollinger, 2008, 24½″ × 33½″

ATTEMPT 1

WHAT IF I start with a unit that is asymmetrical and has no apparent pattern? Four of the units rotated make a Nine-Patch Pinwheel block. Six of the blocks repeated make a quilt.

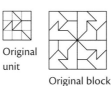

Original unit

Original block

Quilt; block repeated

DO I LIKE IT? It's interesting.

WHY? I see shapes I haven't seen before. I want to try playing with them and see what happens.

ATTEMPT 2

WHAT IF I color it using a series of yellow-greens?

Block with colors

Quilt; blocks repeated

DO I LIKE IT? I enjoy it.

WHY? It's like looking at the nose end of six old-fashioned propeller planes. In my imagination I can see the four-bladed propellers spinning.

ATTEMPT 3

WHAT IF I create a second block by vertically reflecting the Nine-Patch Pinwheel block and then alternating the two blocks in the quilt design?

Block

Vertically reflected block

Quilt; straight and reflected blocks

DO I LIKE IT? Not as much.

WHY? The propeller blades have stopped spinning and are locked together. However, the propeller blades now create an interesting grid.

ATTEMPT 4

WHAT IF I go back to Attempt 2 and vary the colors of all the propeller blades? Then I can rotate the blocks so that the blades are in various positions.

Block with new colors

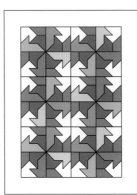

Quilt; each block rotated

DO I LIKE IT? I'm not impressed.

WHY? I thought the color change would keep the eye moving from blade to blade and help simulate spin. It didn't. And it has occurred to me that I don't really want to create a picture of airplanes right now.

ATTEMPT 5

WHAT IF I delete the dark green? This has the effect of removing one of the diagonals from the nine-patch unit.

Original unit

Unit with removed seam

Block

DO I LIKE IT? It's pleasant but not exciting.

WHY? There's not much happening—very little motion. It is simple and a bit calming. Happily, the airplanes are gone.

Quilt; each block rotated

ATTEMPT 6

WHAT IF I add back a smaller amount of the dark green by adding in a new diagonal seam?

Unit

Unit with new diagonal seam

Block

DO I LIKE IT? Same comment as before: It's okay but I'm not excited.

WHY? I'm not sure. Maybe it's too rigid. Maybe it's too repetitive. Maybe it's me not knowing what I want.

Quilt; each block rotated

ATTEMPT 7

WHAT IF I add another small triangle of the dark green?

Unit

Unit with new seams

Block

DO I LIKE IT? Somewhat.

WHY? It's very textural. There is a lot to look at and explore. I even get a feeling of rhythm from the white accents. However, I am more intrigued by the outline of the Nine-Patch Pinwheel block than I am by the colored quilt.

Quilt; each block rotated

ATTEMPT 8

WHAT IF I use the same colors as before but place them differently and add a dark green border?

Block with changed colors

Quilt; new border color, block repeated

DO I LIKE IT? Very much. I've found something I want to make.

WHY? Good question. Maybe because it is so different from what I've been doing. It's very textural. It's calm but it has good variety. It has some movement. The green makes me think of a series of clock dials with the hands in different positions.

ATTEMPT 9

WHAT IF I try a dark brown border?

DO I LIKE IT? Yes.

WHY? Either the green or the brown border would work. I think the brown frames it better. It provides more contrast and makes everything seem a little richer. This is the one.

Quilt; new border color

TAWATINAW

Linda Hurd, 2009, 27½" × 36½"

ATTEMPT 1

WHAT IF I start with this unit? Four units rotated make the Nine-Patch Pinwheel block. Six blocks repeated make the quilt.

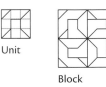

Unit

Block

Quilt; blocks repeated

DO I LIKE IT? I don't dislike it.

WHY? I don't find it terribly exciting, but I think it has some potential. I want to experiment with it.

ATTEMPT 2

WHAT IF I color it white and purple?

Block with color

Quilt; blocks repeated

DO I LIKE IT? I'm not excited.

WHY? This is very static. There is no movement. A couple of years ago I might have been happy with this. But now it's old hat; I want something more.

ATTEMPT 3

WHAT IF I switch some of the purples around and rotate half the blocks?

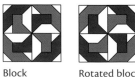

Block

Rotated block

Quilt; straight and rotated blocks

DO I LIKE IT? This is better.

WHY? There is some variety, and there is some movement. But I find the diamond shapes in the center a bit too mundane.

ATTEMPT 4

WHAT IF I alter the purple diamond shapes by adding another horizontal seam?

Original
unit

Unit with new
horizontal seam

Block with
new horizontal
seams

Rotated block

Quilt; straight and rotated blocks

DO I LIKE IT? It's getting better.

WHY? The large purple diamond shapes are gone, the new shapes that replace them in the center are more interesting. I wonder if something else can be done with this new shape.

ATTEMPT 5

WHAT IF I add a seam into this new shape so that I can divide it into two colors?

Unit

Unit with
new vertical
seam

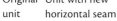
Block with
new vertical
seams

Rotated block

Quilt; straight and rotated blocks

DO I LIKE IT? I don't see much difference.

WHY? The new shape is still the same, only now it is two-toned. In addition, the outside edges of the pattern feel unfinished to me.

ATTEMPT 6

WHAT IF I divide the border in two? I can finish the pattern by joining it back into itself in the first border. I'll leave the second border plain.

Quilt; new border

DO I LIKE IT? This makes a big difference. And I do like it.

WHY? Before, I was looking at a small piece of a much larger object. Now, I am looking at a complete object. Before, the story didn't have an ending; now, it does.

ATTEMPT 7

WHAT IF I color the border brown?

Quilt; new border color

DO I LIKE IT? I don't.

WHY? The border is interfering with the overall shape. Even if the border were much lighter, I think it would still detract from the shape. It would be better to have no border at all.

ATTEMPT 8

WHAT IF I add a third section to the border, making the quilt a little larger? I can create a frame in the second and third borders that doesn't interfere with the pattern.

Quilt; new border in new colors

DO I LIKE IT? This I like.

WHY? The border mimics the shape of the purple pattern and gives it a frame that strengthens it rather than detracts from it.

ATTEMPT 9

WHAT IF I color in the border with black on the outside edge?

Quilt; new border color

DO I LIKE IT? I don't.

WHY? It's too heavy. It's not in harmony with the rest of the image. I like Attempt 8; that's my final answer.

DUCHESS

Wayne Kollinger, 2008, 24½" × 33½"

ATTEMPT 1

WHAT IF I try this for my nine-patch unit, my Nine-Patch Pinwheel block, and my quilt?

Original unit

Original block

Quilt; block repeated

DO I LIKE IT? I do.

WHY? I see all kinds of odd shapes that pop out at me and then disappear. There is no real focus at this point, but there is lots of potential.

ATTEMPT 2

WHAT IF I color the Nine-Patch Pinwheel block in as nontraditional a manner as I can manage, using shades of green and white?

Block

Quilt; block repeated

DO I LIKE IT? Not particularly.

WHY? The pinwheel block is a mess, and the quilt is too. It has some texture but no discernable pattern. I want to see more structure.

ATTEMPT 3

WHAT IF I try rotating the block in all four positions and repeating two of them?

Block

Rotated block

Second rotated block

Third rotated block

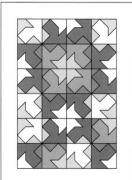

Quilt; rotated blocks

DO I LIKE IT? It's an improvement, but I can't say I like it.

WHY? There is more structure than before. However, the pattern I've created doesn't look quite right; it looks misshapen and incomplete.

ATTEMPT 4

The top four blocks from Attempt 3 form a super-pinwheel (a large pinwheel made of smaller ones) that I like.

WHAT IF I split this and put half at the top of the quilt and half at the bottom?

DO I LIKE IT? Yes, but how should I complete the pattern?

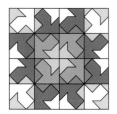

Four-block section

Four-block section split in half

WHAT IF I repeat the Row 2 units in Row 4 and repeat the Row 5 units in Row 3?

Row 2 units

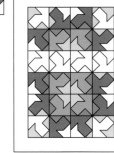

Repeat second row of units in Row 4

Row 5 units

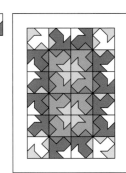

Quilt; repeat fifth row of units in Row 3

DO I LIKE IT? I like it very much.

WHY? It has unity and variety. There are the light green stars at the center, two medium green squarish shapes around them, and the intricate dark green shape around those uniting everything into a single unit. The white negative shape around the outside nicely balances the large green center shape. Every level of this pattern has interest and character. This is a keeper.

ATTEMPT 5

I like it, but can I make it even better?

WHAT IF I finish this quilt with a green border?

DO I LIKE IT? Not as much as I did.

WHY? The border confines the image; it takes away the balancing white shapes. I like the previous one much better.

Quilt; new border color

ATTEMPT 6

WHAT IF I go back to the white border and instead replace the light green in the blocks with a yellow-green?

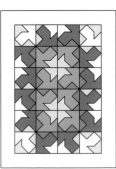

DO I LIKE IT? Absolutely! This is the one I'm going to sew.

WHY? The second color adds another level of interest by creating contrast and emphasizing the center stars. It is livelier than Attempt 4.

Quilt; new border color, new block color

CHAPTER 5:

What Happened?

It's easy to design when you ask, "What if...?" "Do I like it?" and "Why?"

Asking, "What if...?" helps you discover design strategies. Asking, "Why?" helps you discover design principles. You will need both when you design. Let's look at some of the strategies and principles that were used while designing the quilts in the last chapter.

DESIGN STRATEGIES

In general, a strategy is a plan of action aimed at reaching a goal. For our purposes, a design strategy is anything that you try in the process of designing a quilt. Every time you ask, "What if...?" you are in search of a new strategy. Here are a few of the design strategies I used in the last chapter.

Repeat

Many quilts are made by repeating a single quilt block. I start designing a Nine-Patch Pinwheel quilt by repeating a block six times.

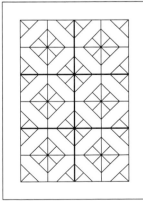

Blocks repeated

Reflect

When repeating a block doesn't create an interesting quilt, I sometimes try reflecting the block to see what happens.

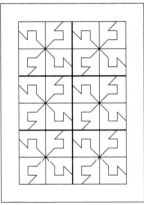

Blocks repeated

Blocks reflected vertically and horizontally

Rotate

I find rotating blocks creates the greatest variety of designs. They can be rotated systematically or randomly. The amount of rotation can vary from block to block, and not all of the blocks need to be rotated. The results will depend to a large extent on the way the blocks are colored.

Blocks repeated

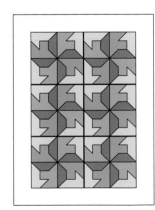

Blocks rotated

Mixing repeated, reflected, and rotated blocks can result in some quite surprising patterns.

Divide

You can divide large areas into smaller ones to add complexity. The opposite strategy is also possible; you can consolidate smaller areas into larger ones.

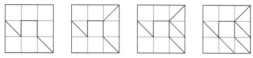

Step-by-step division of a unit

Compare

Color can dramatically change a pattern. You may want to try several color variations of a design, then compare them to find the one that suits you.

Color options

Add

In the example below, more color was added to give the design some life. You could also add more blocks to make a larger quilt. Adding a border that complements or completes the design can be very effective.

Add more color

Match

By matching colors, you can blend different areas together. In the example, the border and background are united by a common color (see *Lac Des Arcs*, page 27).

Cohesive background and border color

Restart

Sometimes, if a design is going nowhere, you have to eliminate all the color in the pattern and start again.

Remove color and start over

For more strategies, reread Chapter 4, paying special attention to the answers to the question "What if...?" Also notice that it doesn't take a genius to devise these strategies. When you design, you can start with these, but you will soon find yourself inventing more of your own.

DESIGN PRINCIPLES

Design principles are general rules of design. They help you decide how to make a design work. You discover design principles by asking "Why?" Here are a few.

Contrast Separates

Notice how the increased contrast of the white with the green separates the pinwheels from the background.

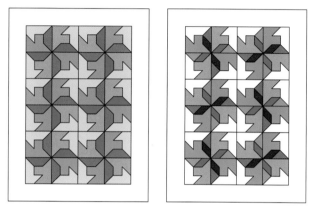

Contrasting colors separate elements.

Similar colors unify elements.

Similarity Unifies

Similar colors unify design elements. Notice how the reds read as one element in the photo below, and how the green parts unite to become one element and the red parts unite to become another in the next photo.

Similar colors unify elements.

Black Intensifies

Colors that are next to black become more intense. In the example the black makes the orange and the green seem richer and deeper.

Black makes other colors more intense.

Variety Creates Interest

The illustration on the left uses dark purple for the foreground pinwheels and light purple in the background diamonds. Varying this, by putting some of the dark purple into the background and some of the light purple into the foreground, makes the quilt more interesting.

Moving colors around creates interest.

Too Much Variety Is Confusing

When too much is happening in a quilt, it becomes unfocused and confusing. In the example, the structure breaks down because there is too much variation in the coloring of the rectangles.

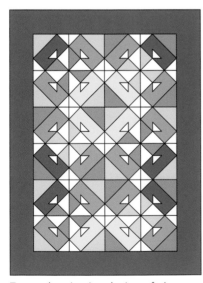

Too much variety in color is confusing.

Unity Fosters Identity

The illustration on the left is unorganized. The design elements are not unified; they do not come together to make anything. In the illustration on the right, the design elements unite to create a form. It is something; it has an identity.

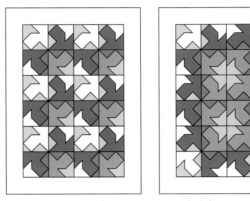

Arrangement can unify design elements (right).

For more design principles, reread Chapter 4, paying special attention to the answers to the question "Why?" As you design, you will discover even more principles, some of which will be unique to you. The more design principles you know and understand, the easier it is to design.

LOOKING FOR STRATEGIES AND PRINCIPLES

Quilters are always looking for something new. Sometimes this means a new pattern or technique, sometimes a new fabric or gadget. What quilt designers look for are new design strategies.

Ideas and inspiration are everywhere—in books and magazines, at guild meetings and quilt shows. When I meet a new quilt, I ask myself three questions: **"Do I like it?" "Why?"** and **"What if…?"** The answer to the question **"What if…?"** is often a new strategy that I can file for future reference.

Looking for design principles is trickier. The authors of design books do not agree on what design principles are, so each has a different list. This can be confusing.

I suggest you take a practical approach. If something helps you answer the question, "Why do I like it or not like it?" add it to your list of design principles. Your experience is your best guide. It's you that your quilts have to please.

PART 2:

WHAT NEXT?

Design has a split personality. Sometimes it's art; sometimes it's engineering.

Part 1 was about playing with visual elements—things like color, shape, and symmetry—in order to create a design for an original quilt (that's the art part). But you want to create more than a design; you want to create a quilt. Before you can start sewing, you need to do some planning. You need to decide how to turn the dream into reality (that's the engineering part).

An engineer provides a client with three things: blueprints, specifications, and supervision. In order to sew a quilt you've designed, you will need all three. As a quilter, you already have experience supervising yourself while constructing quilts. As a designer, you also need to provide your client (that's you, too) with a blueprint (a pattern to work from) and specifications (a list of materials with instructions on what to do with them). Part 2 is about how to do that.

CHAPTER 6

Pattern Planning

Even though quilts differ, the process for turning a design into a pattern is the same, in general, for all quilts.

1. Divide the design into large manageable pieces. Then divide those large pieces into smaller and smaller pieces. Keep track of the stages so you can reverse the order to sew the quilt.

2. Group together any pieces that are the same (in color and/or size and/or pattern). This reduces the number of items that you need to deal with.

3. Determine the size of the pieces.

4. Calculate the amount of fabric needed.

I'm going to use the finished quilt *Duchess* to demonstrate the process.

Duchess, Wayne Kollinger, 2008, 24½″ × 33½″

DIVIDE THE QUILT TOP INTO BLOCKS

Rather than try to deal with the whole quilt top all at once, divide it into large pieces that can be dealt with one at a time. For the moment we'll ignore the border and deal with it later. This quilt is easily divided into six Nine-Patch Pinwheel blocks.

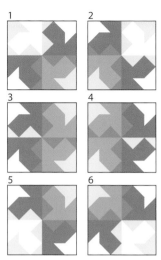

Six blocks

To make life simpler, gather the blocks into groups.

By rotating Blocks 2, 5, and 6, you discover that they are identical to Block 1. Call this Block AA.

By rotating Block 4, you discover that it is identical to Block 3. Call this Block BB.

Block AA; there are 4.

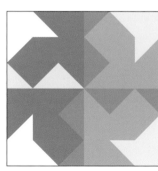

Block BB; there are 2.

DIVIDE THE BLOCKS INTO UNITS

Next, divide the blocks into smaller pieces.

Block AA can be divided into 4 units, and each unit is different. Call them Units A, B, C, and D. Since there are 4 AA blocks in the quilt *Duchess*, it takes 4 each of Units A, B, C, and D to make the AA blocks.

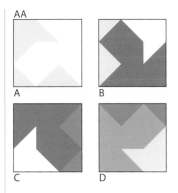

Block AA: Four units; A, B, C, D

Similarly, Block BB can be divided into 4 units. These are repeats of the Units B, C, and D used to make Block AA. Unit D is used twice in Block BB. Since there are 2 BB blocks in the quilt *Duchess*, it takes 2 each of Units B and C and 4 of Unit D to make the BB blocks.

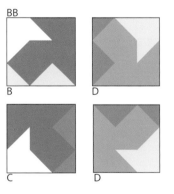

Block BB: Four units; B, C, D

To find the total number of each unit contained in the quilt *Duchess*, add the number of those units in Block AA to those in Block BB. The result is 4 of Unit A, 6 of Unit B, 6 of Unit C, and 8 of Unit D.

TREATING THE UNITS AS ONE

When the color is removed from the A, B, C, and D units, they become the same unit. This is the basic *Duchess* quilt nine-patch unit. When this basic unit is divided into even smaller pieces, the results can be applied to the four original units.

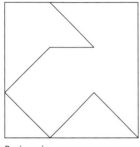

Basic unit

Divide the Basic Unit into Sub-Units

There is more than one method you can use to divide a unit. You need to discover which way works best for you. You can use the design process to do this. But instead of asking, "Do I like it?" (an aesthetic question), you ask, "Does it work?" (a practical question).

Method 1

WHAT IF the unit is divided into the squares of the original nine-patch grid?

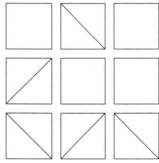

Unit divided into squares

DOES IT WORK? Yes and no.

WHY? This has the advantage of simplicity; only one size of square has to be cut, and half-square triangles can be mass-produced using your favorite method. But there are 14 component pieces; this is more than any other method. That means more cutting and more sewing.

Method 2

WHAT IF the unit is divided into 3 vertical strip sub-units?

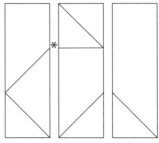

Unit divided into vertical strips

DOES IT WORK? Yes and no.

WHY? There are now 9 pieces. But there could be a problem matching seams at point *.

Method 3

WHAT IF the unit is divided into 3 horizontal strip sub-units?

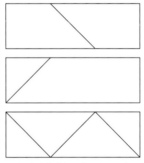

Unit divided into horizontal strips

DOES IT WORK? Yes and no.

WHY? There are 8 pieces, but there could be fewer. There are no problems matching seams. All the pieces can be cut from strips. This will make cutting easy and will simplify calculating the amount of fabric needed.

Method 4

WHAT IF the units are divided directly into pieces rather than sub-units?

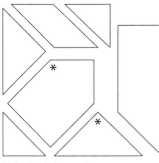

Unit divided into pieces

DOES IT WORK? Yes and no.

WHY? There are only 7 pieces, and there are no problems matching seams. However, there are inset seams at *. I prefer to avoid inset seams.

Method 5

WHAT IF the unit is divided into different pieces?

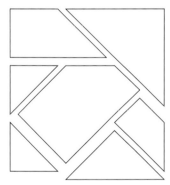

Unit divided into different pieces

DOES IT WORK? Yes and no.

WHY? There are still only 7 pieces, and the inset seams are gone. There are no problems matching seams. However, the pieces are all different sizes; they have to be sized and cut individually. Sewing time is at a minimum, but cutting time is at a maximum. It will also be more difficult, and take longer, to calculate the fabric needed.

So What Does Work?

You would expect the answer to "Does it work?" to be either yes or no. Sometimes it is. But often it depends on who asks the question.

There's too much sewing for me in Method 1, but you might like the idea of sewing the unit like a Nine-Patch block. I shy away from the inset seams in Method 4, but for you they may be as easy as eating chocolate. Each of us has different skills. What works for one doesn't work for another. We end up doing things differently, but we both do what works best.

In the case of this basic unit for the quilt *Duchess*, I like Method 3, so that's the version we will proceed with.

Divide Sub-Units into Pieces

Divide each horizontal strip sub-unit into pieces along the seams.

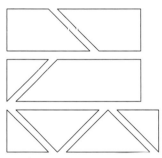

Divide strip sub-units at seams.

I don't like dealing with triangles, so I convert all the pieces to either squares or rectangles. I create the triangles by sewing diagonal seams within my squares or rectangles, using the method described on page 64 (see Diagonal Seams).

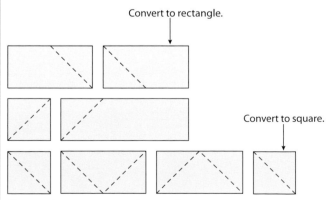

Convert to rectangle.

Convert to square.

Convert pieces to squares and rectangles.

DETERMINING SIZES

The nine-patch unit for *Duchess* was designed on a nine-patch grid. As a result, it can be made using pieces of only 3 sizes. Each finished piece is equal to either 1, 2, or 3 squares of the original nine-patch grid.

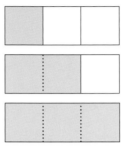

Finished pieces cover 1, 2, or 3 squares of the grid.

The actual size of the pieces is determined by choosing a size for the grid.

You need to decide how big a quilt you want and how small a piece you are comfortable working with. To do this, ask "What if...?" What if the grid squares are 3″ × 3″? What if they are 1″ × 1″? Then calculate the size of a unit, a block, and a quilt and see if you like the results.

For the quilts in this book, I settled on a grid with 1½″ × 1½″ squares. Because they must fit the grid, finished pieces (using square or rectangular dimensions) are either 1½″ × 1½″, 1½″ × 3″, or 1½″ × 4½″. (That is, the finished pieces fit into a box with one of these sizes.)

Add ¼″ seam allowances on all sides to these finished sizes, and the pieces are cut 2″ × 2″, 2″ × 3½″, or 2″ × 5″.

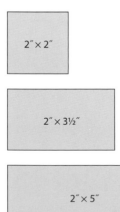

2″ × 2″

2″ × 3½″

2″ × 5″

Pieces are only three sizes.

The size of the grid squares determines the size of everything else.

For *Duchess*, since the grid squares are 1½″ × 1½″, the nine-patch grid is 4½″ × 4½″, so that is the finished size of a nine-patch unit.

Four nine-patch units make a block, so the block is 9″ × 9″ finished.

A quilt that is 2 by 3 blocks is 18″ × 27″, not including borders.

The overall size of the quilt now depends on the size of the borders. In the case of *Duchess*, this means adding 3¼″ all around, making the quilt top 24½″ × 33½″ without binding.

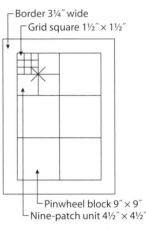

Border 3¼″ wide
Grid square 1½″ × 1½″

Pinwheel block 9″ × 9″
Nine-patch unit 4½″ × 4½″

Grid square size determines everything else.

BORDERS

Duchess has plain borders that measure 3¼″ wide without binding. This is a simple situation to deal with.

Sometimes a design needs more than plain borders. If your quilt has pieced borders, you will need to create a pattern for the borders as well. You do that by following the same procedure as for the quilt top—divide it into smaller and smaller pieces.

OTHER QUILTS

Not every quilt you design is going to use nine-patch grid blocks. Nor is every quilt you design going to be made with blocks. How do you divide up a quilt that isn't made with blocks based on a nine-patch grid?

You use the design process. An entire quilt can be divided up in the same way that the basic nine-patch unit was divided up on page 46. Ask, "What if...?" "Does it work?" and "Why?" and search for the best way to divide the quilt into large sections. Do this again and divide those large sections into smaller units. Keep repeating the process until you get down to the individual pieces.

CHAPTER 7:
How Much Fabric?

In theory, calculating fabric is simple. Add all the little pieces together to find how much you need of each color. In practice, it's almost that simple. However, the number of pieces you need to add can make it look complicated. Focus on small units, and the job becomes easy.

Let's determine how much fabric is required for the quilt *Duchess* (page 44) to see how it's done.

CALCULATE THE FABRIC REQUIRED FOR EACH UNIT

Unit A

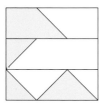

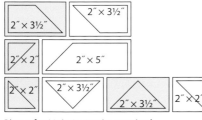

Pieces for Unit A; 4 units required

How much white fabric is needed to make 1 Unit A? All the pieces are cut 2″ wide. Add the lengths of all the white pieces together, and you find you need a strip of fabric 2″ × 14″ (3½″ + 5″ + 3½″ + 2″ = 14″).

How much white fabric is needed to make all 4 of Unit A in *Duchess*? Multiply by 4 and you find you need a strip of fabric 2″ × 56″ (4 × 14″ = 56″). The top chart summarizes the calculations for all the required white pieces.

WHITE PIECES IN UNIT A

Color	Size of Pieces	Number of Pieces	Size × Number of Pieces = Length	Number of A Units	Length × Number of A Units = Total Length Required
White	2″ × 2″	1	2″ × 2″		
	2″ × 3½″	2	2″ × 7″		
	2″ × 5″	1	2″ × 5″		
Total for all white pieces			2″ × 14″	4	2″ × 56″

Now do the same for the yellow-green fabric in Unit A.

YELLOW-GREEN PIECES IN UNIT A

Color	Size of Pieces	Number of Pieces	Size × Number of Pieces = Length	Number of A Units	Length × Number of A Units = Total Length Required
Yellow-green	2″ × 2″	2	2″ × 4″		
	2″ × 3½″	2	2″ × 7″		
Total for all yellow-green pieces			2″ × 11″	4	2″ × 44″

Proceed to do the same for Units B, C, and D.

Unit B

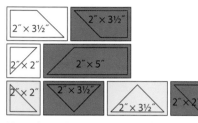

Pieces for Unit B; 6 units required

PIECES IN UNIT B

Color	Size of Pieces	Number of Pieces	Size × Number of Pieces = Length	Number of B Units	Length × Number of B Units = Total Length Required
White	2″ × 2″	1	2″ × 2″		
	2″ × 3½″	1	2″ × 3½″		
Total for all white pieces			2″ × 5½″	6	2″ × 33″
Yellow-green	2″ × 2″	1	2″ × 2″		
	2″ × 3½″	1	2″ × 3½″		
Total for all yellow-green pieces			2″ × 5½″	6	2″ × 33″
Dark green	2″ × 2″	1	2″ × 2″		
	2″ × 3½″	2	2″ × 7″		
	2″ × 5″	1	2″ × 5″		
Total for all dark green pieces			2″ × 14″	6	2″ × 84″

Unit C

Pieces for Unit C; 6 units required

PIECES IN UNIT C

Color	Size of Pieces	Number of Pieces	Size × Number of Pieces = Length	Number of C Units	Length × Number of C Units = Total Length Required
White	2″ × 2″	1	2″ × 2″		
	2″ × 3½″	1	2″ × 3½″		
Total for all white pieces			2″ × 5½″	6	2″ × 33″
Medium green	2″ × 2″	1	2″ × 2″		
	2″ × 3½″	1	2″ × 3½″		
Total for all medium green pieces			2″ × 5½″	6	2″ × 33″
Dark green	2″ × 2″	1	2″ × 2″		
	2″ × 3½″	2	2″ × 7″		
	2″ × 5″	1	2″ × 5″		
Total for all dark green pieces			2″ × 14″	6	2″ × 84″

Unit D

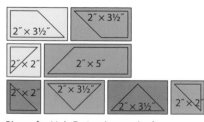

Pieces for Unit D; 8 units required

PIECES IN UNIT D

Color	Size of Pieces	Number of Pieces	Size × Number of Pieces = Length	Number of D Units	Length × Number of D Units = Total Length Required
Yellow-green	2″ × 2″	1	2″ × 2″		
	2″ × 3½″	1	2″ × 3½″		
Total for all yellow-green pieces			2″ × 5½″	8	2″ × 44″
Medium green	2″ × 2″	1	2″ × 2″		
	2″ × 3½″	1	2″ × 3½″		
Total for all medium green pieces			2″ × 5½″	8	2″ × 44″
Light green	2″ × 2″	1	2″ × 2″		
	2″ × 3½″	2	2″ × 7″		
	2″ × 5″	1	2″ × 5″		
Total for all light green pieces			2″ × 14″	8	2″ × 112″

ADD THE TOTALS

The next step is to calculate the total amount of each fabric you need for the quilt top. Take the amounts needed for each color within each unit from the tables and add them together.

White	Yellow-Green	Light Green	Medium Green	Dark Green
Unit A = 2″ × 56″	Unit A = 2″ × 44″	Unit D = 2″ × 112″	Unit C = 2″ × 33″	Unit B = 2″ × 84″
Unit B = 2″ × 33″	Unit B = 2″ × 33″	Total = 2″ × 112″	Unit D = 2″ × 44″	Unit C = 2″ × 84″
Unit C = 2″ × 33″	Unit D = 2″ × 44″		Total = 2″ × 77″	Total = 2″ × 168″
Total = 2″ × 122″	Total = 2″ × 121″			

ADD THE BORDER AND BINDING

We still need a border. The border on the quilt *Duchess* is white. It requires 2 pieces 3½″ × 18½″ and 2 pieces 3½″ × 33½″. The 2 pieces 18½″ long can be cut from 1 strip of fabric 40″ long. The 2 pieces 33½″ long are cut from 2 separate strips. It follows that we need 3 strips, each 3½″ wide. Since 3 × 3½″ = 10½″, a piece of white fabric 10¼″ × 40″ is needed for the border and is then added to the total for white fabric.

If it were a pieced border, then a calculation, like that for the units, would need to be made and those results added to the totals.

Finally, there's the binding. The binding on *Duchess* is also white. How much fabric is required depends on the binding method you use. In this case, with no mitered corners, I would allow for a minimum 2″ × 130″ strip , or ¼ yard. This amount is added to the total for white fabric. In this book, the binding is not included as part of the design process for the quilt tops. You will need to add extra yardage to finish your quilt to include batting, backing, and binding.

Using the general method described above, you can figure the theoretical length needed for strips of any width. I say theoretical because fabric doesn't come in endless strips. You still need to do one of the following two calculations to convert strip length into yardage.

BUYING FABRIC

When you buy fabric, it usually comes about 40″ wide. You need to calculate how many 40″ strips of each color you need.

For *Duchess*, you need 2″ × 168″ of dark green. How many 40″ strips is that? When 168″ is divided by 40″ the result is 4.2, so 5 strips are needed (always round up to the next whole number). The strips are 2″ wide, so you will need a minimum of 10″ of dark green fabric (2″ × 5 = 10″).

When you are cutting out the pieces, you may find that they don't always fit exactly into a 40″ strip. To allow for this and the occasional "oops," *you should always buy extra fabric*. I suggest buying at least enough for another strip or two. You should also round up your calculations to the nearest ⅛ or ⅙ yard, which is how the fabric will be cut at your favorite quilt shop. Remember, any leftovers can be added to your stash and used in your next quilt.

USING YOUR STASH

Why buy fabric when you've got a stash? Keep in mind that the pieces of fabric in your stash could be any size. That means doing a slightly different calculation.

For *Duchess*, you need 2″ × 112″ of light green. Will a piece of light green that is 13″ × 20″ work? When 112″ (the total length needed) is divided by 20″ (the length of the piece of light green), the result is 5.6, so 6 strips are needed (always round up to the next whole number). The strips are 2″ wide, and since 2″ × 6 = 12″, you need a piece of light green fabric at least 12″ × 20″. The 13″ × 20″ piece might be big enough if nothing goes wrong. But to allow for squaring up, cutting mistakes, and waste, I would look for a larger piece of light green fabric.

PART 3:

WHAT ELSE?

Now that you know how to design Nine-Patch Pinwheel quilts, you will want to move on to bigger and better things—and rightly so.

So how do you do that? How do you go from designing simple Nine-Patch Pinwheel quilts to designing anything and everything you set your mind to? Part 3 will show you how you can expand your design horizons, one step at a time. The first step is to do more with a Nine-Patch Pinwheel quilt design.

CHAPTER 8:
More Blocks, Please

A quilt can be any size, from as small as a potholder or a placemat to as large as a queen-size quilt or larger. Let's explore some ways to resize Nine-Patch Pinwheel quilts.

WHAT IF A QUILT WERE A BLOCK?

If the quilt *Duchess* (page 44) were treated like a block instead of a quilt, then it could be repeated to make a larger quilt. *Summer in Duchess* was made using nine *Duchess* quilts/blocks.

Duchess quilts/blocks

Summer in Duchess, Linda Hurd, 2008, 78″ × 102″

North Cooking Lake is another typical Nine-Patch Pinwheel quilt. Use it as a quilt/block and rotate it, and the lap quilt version is the result.

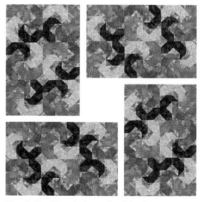

North Cooking Lake quilts/blocks

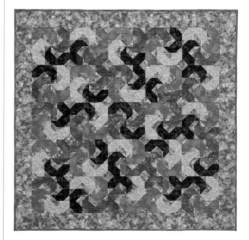

North Cooking Lake Lap Quilt, Wayne Kollinger, 2009, 51″ × 51″

WHAT IF NINE-PATCH PINWHEEL BLOCKS ARE USED DIFFERENTLY?

Two Nine-Patch Pinwheel blocks from *Mirror* (page 72) were used to make the placemat.

Mirror block

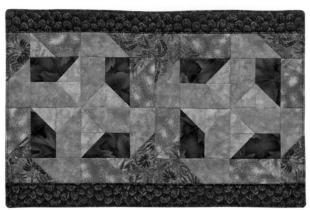

Mirror Placemat, Linda Hurd, 2008, 12″ × 18″

This table runner was made using four of the *Tawatinaw* Nine-Patch Pinwheel blocks (page 74).

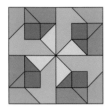

Tawatinaw block

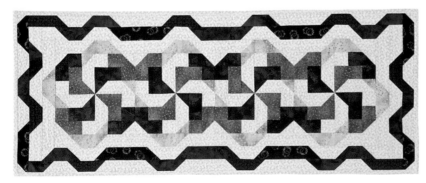

Tawatinaw Table Runner, Linda Hurd, 2008, 18″ × 45″

Two versions of the *Tees* Nine-Patch Pinwheel blocks (page 68) using different greens were combined to make a border for this crib quilt.

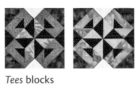

Tees blocks

Tees Crib Quilt, Wayne Kollinger, 2009, 39″ × 66″

WHAT IF NINE-PATCH UNITS ARE USED DIFFERENTLY?

The placemat was made using two of the nine-patch units for *Mirror* (page 72).

Mirror block

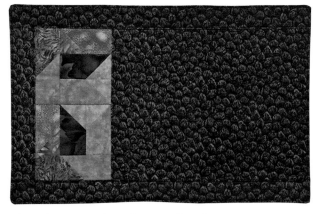

Mirror Placemat, Linda Hurd, 2008, 12″ × 18″

WHAT IF ONLY PART OF THE QUILT IS USED?

If the top two Nine-Patch Pinwheel blocks are left off *Lac Des Arcs* (page 70), the result is *Lac Des Arcs Table Quilt*.

Lac Des Arcs quilt

Lac Des Arcs Table Quilt, Wayne Kollinger, 2008, 24″ × 24″

WHAT IF PART OF THE QUILT IS USED AS A BLOCK?

If the top two Nine-Patch Pinwheel blocks are left off of *Orion* (page 66), then the result is a new large block that forms an O. If the bottom two Nine-Patch Pinwheel blocks are left off *Orion*, the result is a new large block that forms an X. Both of these new large blocks were used to make the queen-size quilt.

Section of *Orion*

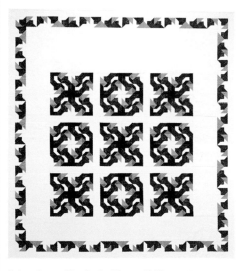

Orion Queen-Size Quilt, Wayne Kollinger, 2009, 98″ × 102″, quilted by Linda Hurd

The design process doesn't have to end once you've created a standard six-block Nine-Patch Pinwheel quilt. Use your design as your starting point and begin the design process all over again. You can ask, "What if…?" "Do I like it?" and "Why?" and create something even more wonderful.

CHAPTER 9:
New Games

This book is about a design process. In order to demonstrate that process, I introduced Nine-Patch Pinwheel quilts. But you don't have to design Nine-Patch Pinwheel quilts to use the design process. You can design all kinds of quilts.

I treated designing Nine-Patch Pinwheel quilts as a game, defined the rules, and then applied the design process. You can do that with other quilts. You can make a game of Log Cabin quilts, crazy quilts, Hawaiian quilts, Star quilts—any kind of quilt you can think of—and come up with your own designs.

But you can do even more than that. What if, instead of just playing one of these quilt games, you changed it? What if you looked at the rules and asked, "What if...?" "Do I like it?" and "Why?" Instead of designing a quilt you would be designing a quilt game, and the result would be an endless number of new and original quilts.

In this book, there isn't room to explore even a fraction of the possibilities. I am going to let you do the exploring. However, we can look at the rules for the Nine-Patch Pinwheel game and explore some of the strategies you might use to change them. No doubt you will be able to think of many more.

Rule #1: Designs start on a nine-patch grid with a mandatory half-square triangle whose diagonal runs into the corner.

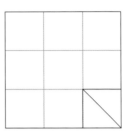

- What if the mandatory half-square triangle is eliminated?

- What if the grid is a four-patch grid? Or a sixteen-patch?

- What if designs are based on a Pinwheel or a Log Cabin block?

Rule #2: Designs are made using only squares and half-square triangles. These can be placed anywhere in the grid and arranged in any way.

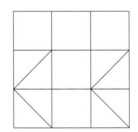

- What if only plain squares are used in the center squares of the grid?

- What if some or all of the following squares are used?

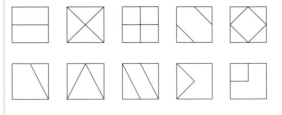

Rule #3: Unnecessary seams can be eliminated unless you want to sew them.

This rule is optional, which means that it isn't really a rule at all. It's hard to change a rule that doesn't exist.

Rule #4: Four nine-patch units are arranged with their mandatory half-square triangles touching to make a Nine-Patch Pinwheel block.

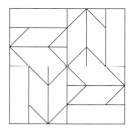

- What if the nine-patch units are reflected instead of rotated?
- What if a four-patch unit is used to make a pinwheel?
- What if Log Cabin blocks are used to make a Nine-Patch block?

Rule #5: Color the nine-patch units any way you like.

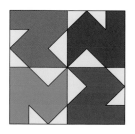

- What if they are all colored the same?
- What if none of them are colored the same?
- What if one of the blocks must be colored red?

Rule #6: Six Nine-Patch Pinwheel blocks with a border make a Nine-Patch Pinwheel quilt.

In Chapter 8 (pages 53–55), we saw what can happen when this rule is changed.

Rule #7: Color the Nine-Patch Pinwheel blocks any way you like.

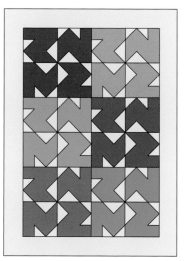

- What if they are all colored the same?
- What if the blocks at the top of the quilt are colored lighter than those at the bottom?
- What if every quilt is a checkerboard?

Rule #8: Nine-Patch Pinwheel blocks can be repeated, reflected, or rotated.

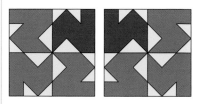
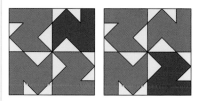

- What if every quilt has to include a repeated, a reflected, and a rotated block?
- What if half the blocks are repeated and half are rotated?
- What if every block is simply repeated?

When you design, where you start doesn't matter. Where you start is merely the first in a series of steps that lead to a new design. What matters is where you end up. What matters is having a quilt of your own design.

CHAPTER 10:
New Adventures

In Chapter 1, I told you to treat quilt design as a treasure hunt and go looking for treasure. So far we've been hunting treasure without any goal in mind, except to find something.

In this chapter we're going to look at hunting with a specific goal in mind. To do this you must ask important questions before you start: "What am I looking for? What do I want?"

"Do I want to design a pieced quilt or an appliqué quilt?" "Do I want to design a picture quilt or a pattern quilt?" "Do I want to design lettering for a quilt?" "Do I want to design a quilted tote bag?" There are lots of possibilities.

Let's take one last look at the design process to see how asking "What do I want?" changes it.

Okotoks/Falling, Wayne Kollinger, 2007, 24½" × 33½"

Enchant, Wayne Kollinger, 2005, 24½" × 33½"

THE DESIGN PROCESS—
NEW AND IMPROVED

What Do I Want?

The new question "What do I want?" comes first. It is about choosing goals.

Do you want to make a lap quilt for Aunt Martha or a crib quilt for young Caitlin? Or maybe you want to experiment with an art quilt for yourself. Once you know your goal, you can start designing.

You can be as vague or as specific about your goal as you wish. You may only know you want to design a lap quilt of some description for Aunt Martha. Or you may already know that it needs to be a pieced quilt, 40" × 60", in dusty rose floral fabrics.

Don't be afraid to change your mind about what you want while you design. If the teddy bears with balloons aren't working for Caitlin's quilt, you may decide you want bunnies with toy blocks instead. But don't change your mind too often or you'll never finish.

What If...?

The next question, "What if...?", remains the same. This is a creative question. It's about exploring the possibilities.

The things you try by asking, "What if...?" are your design strategies. The more what-ifs you ask, the more design strategies you can try. The more design strategies you try, the more varied and interesting your designs become. The holy grail of design is to ask what-ifs that no one else ever asked and create designs that no one else ever created.

Manyberries, Wayne Kollinger, 2006, 24½" × 33½"

Brook/Pinwheels, Wayne Kollinger, 2008, 24½" × 33½"

Anthracite 2, Linda Hurd, 2007, 24½" × 33½"

Linden/Windows, Wayne Kollinger, 2007, 24½" × 33½"

Do I Like It?

"Do I like it?" is really three questions wrapped up in one: "Is it attractive?" "Is it what I want?" and "Does it work?" If it doesn't work, or it's not what you want, or it's not attractive, you won't like it. You have to be able to answer yes to these three questions before you have a quilt design you want to sew.

"Is it attractive?" is what we were really asking when we asked, "Do I like it?" at the beginning of the book. It is an aesthetic question. It's about style. Style is your way of doing things; it is the result of making decisions about what you like.

"Is it what I want?" is about relevance. Are the things you're trying helping you do what you want to do?

Sometimes asking, "Is it what I want?" can change what you want. Your bunny for Caitlin looks more like a puppy with big ears, but it is cute—very cute. It isn't what you wanted, but when you ask, "Is it what I want?" the answer comes back, "It is now."

"Does it work?" is a practical question. We started asking this in Part 2, the section on planning to sew.

Another way of asking, "Does it work?" is to ask, "Can I make this work?" or "Can I sew this?" As we saw in Part 2, the answer to this changes from person to person.

Galahad, Wayne Kollinger, 2009, 24½" × 33½"

Czar, Marie McEachern, 2006, 24½" × 33½"

Why?

"Why" is also three questions wrapped up in one: "Why is it (not) attractive?" "Why is it (not) what I want?" and "Why does it (not) work?"

"Why is it (not) attractive?" takes you on a search for design principles. You are looking for reasons a design is or isn't attractive. You are looking for general rules that will help you find ways to make it attractive. The more design rules you understand, the easier it is to create something beautiful.

"Why is it (not) what I want?" takes you on a search for appropriateness. You are looking for the ways in which a design is or isn't what you want it to be. This helps you decide what to keep and what to change.

What is appropriate depends very much on what you want. Do you want something that looks like a photograph of a beagle? Do you want something that looks like a cartoon of a beagle? Or do you want something that just looks like some kind of dog?

The better you know your subject matter, the easier it is to design. If you don't know what a beagle looks like, it's hard to design an image of one.

"Why does it (not) work?" takes you on a search for techniques. You are looking for ways to sew your design. The more techniques you know, the more you can achieve as a designer. This doesn't mean you have to know every possible technique before you can design. It means that as a designer you will want to learn more techniques.

DO IT

I want you to design quilts; that's why I wrote this book. You want to design quilts; that's why you bought this book. What if you just go ahead and do it?

An infinite number of quilts are possible. You can make some of them real. They will be quilts designed by you, sewn by you, and loved by you.

Six Projects

Let's turn the demonstrations into quilts!

All six of the quilts in this appendix are part of my Alberta series. I name all of my Nine-Patch Pinwheel quilts after towns in the province of Alberta, Canada. I do this, in part, to show appreciation for my home province. But also because I've designed a lot of quilts and it's an easy way to come up with new names.

I enjoyed designing these quilts. I hope you enjoy sewing them.

BEFORE YOU BEGIN

Fabric Selection

Choosing fabrics is very much a part of the design process. When you are auditioning fabrics for a quilt, asking "What if...?" "Do I like it?" and "Why?" can help you make better choices.

Fabric Mock-Up

Chances are that the fabrics you pick won't match the colors in a project exactly. They may even be very different. Keeping track of what goes where can be a problem. Why not create a mock-up?

The example shows a mock-up of the *Mirror* nine-patch unit (page 73), using fabrics different from those shown in the pattern. Pieces of fabric were cut to size and attached to a copy of the basic mirror block. The pieces were then numbered with a marking pen to match those shown in the color placement diagram.

This is a handy reference to have for both cutting and sewing.

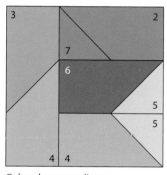
Color placement diagram

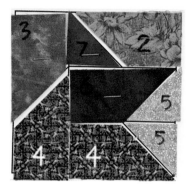
Fabric mock-up

Cutting

All the blocks for the quilts in the Appendix are made using pieces of only three sizes: 2″ × 2″, 2″ × 3½″, and 2″ × 5″. Since all the pieces are 2″ wide, the first thing you need to do is cut the fabric into 2″ strips.

How many strips do you need for each fabric? The cutting chart for each project has a column labeled "Total Length of 2″ Strips." You can use this to calculate the number of strips you need.

For example, the quilt *Orion* needs a 2″ strip of black fabric 90″ long. Fabric comes on bolts about 40″ wide. Divide 90″ by 40″, and you get 2.25. Round up, and you need to cut 3 strips.

Look again at the cutting chart for *Orion* and you will see a column labeled "Yardage," which shows two things. First, it shows the minimum amount of black fabric you need: 6″ × 40″ (3 strips × 2″ wide is 6″). Second, it shows how much fabric to buy: ¼ yard, which is 9″. The extra fabric allows for squaring up and the occasional "oops".

What if you want to use a piece of fabric that isn't 40″ wide? Measure how wide it is and divide that into the length of the 2″ strip you need. Suppose you need a 2″ × 90″ strip and you find a piece of fabric 15″ × 17″ in your stash. Can you use it? Divide 90″ by 17″ and you get 5.29, so you need 6 strips 17″ long.

Each strip is 2″ wide, so you need a piece of fabric 12″ × 17″. You can use the 15″ × 17″ piece, but there won't be much extra for squaring up, cutting mistakes, and waste. Most likely the pieces you cut won't add up to exactly 17″. You may want to look for a larger piece.

SEWING

Everyone has different tastes and talents. So it's not surprising that no two people sew exactly the same way. I'm not going to presume to tell you how you should sew. I'm just going to tell you how I sew. Then you can do what you choose. No doubt you were going to anyway.

Sewing Nine-Patch Pinwheel Units

Straight Seams

When sewing squares to rectangles, sew scant ¼″ seams. When fabric is folded at a seam, some of its width is lost in the fold. A seam that is very slightly less than ¼″ will compensate for this.

If a scant ¼″ seam is too scant, making a joined strip unit too long, you can rip out the seam and resew it, or you can trim the ends. I usually trim. (Strip units are further discussed in the individual projects in this appendix).

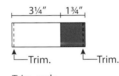

Trim ends.

Press seams within strip units open, unless there is a reason not to.

However, when sewing two strip units together, you can press the seam to one side. I choose the side that offers the least resistance, and I always press the same seam to the same side in all the blocks.

Diagonal Seams

Whether sewing squares to squares, squares to rectangles, or rectangles to rectangles on the diagonal, I always follow the same procedure.

1. Draw the diagonal on the back of the top piece. With squares, this is easy—you draw a line diagonally from one corner to the opposite corner. When you are joining 2 rectangles, an imaginary square is formed where they

overlap. Draw a line diagonally in this square from the corner of the top piece (Point **A** in the next illustration) to the corner of the bottom piece (Point **B**).

2. Align the 2 pieces, with right sides together, and check that the diagonal goes in the right direction.

3. Sew the seam starting at Point **A**. At Point **A**, the corner of the top piece is supported by the bottom piece. I don't start at Point **B** because the corner of the bottom piece is unsupported and could be pushed into the machine by a dull needle.

Sew the seam on the outside of the line but touching it. You should still see the line after the seam is sewn. I do this to compensate for width lost in the fold.

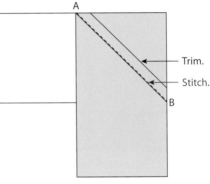

Sew on outside of line.

4. Check that the diagonal goes in the right direction. Then trim, leaving a ¼″ seam allowance.

5. Press the seams open unless there is a reason not to.

Sewing Pinwheel Blocks

A Pinwheel block has eight seams that meet at the center. Some quilters have no trouble with this. I'm not one of them; sometimes I get a great big nasty lump in the middle. To avoid the lump, I don't sew the last ¼″ of the seams at the center where they meet. The loose ends can then be fanned out, forming a small pinwheel and no lump.

Fan center seam allowances.

Here's how it's done.

1. Place 4 nine-patch units in position. Each has a corner diagonal seam that runs into the center of the pinwheel.

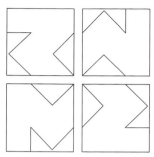

Position units

2. Pick 2 adjacent units and place them with their right sides (the front is the right side) together. Check the corner diagonals to be sure they are positioned one over the other. This corner is where you start sewing.

3. Start ¼" in from the top and side of the units. The needle enters in the diagonal seams of both units, lining them up and ensuring accurate points. Sew a scant ¼" seam.

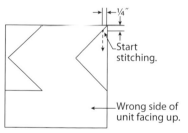

Begin sewing ¼" from both edges.

4. Press the seam to one side. Which side doesn't matter, but it must always be the same side for all the blocks.

5. Repeat Steps 2, 3, and 4 with the other 2 nine-patch units.

6. Place the 2 new units right sides together. The 2 center seams lie in opposite directions and help align the units.

7. Start at the center and sew one-half of the seam. Then start at the center again and sew the other half.

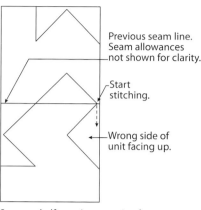

Sew one-half at a time, starting from center each time.

8. Place the completed Pinwheel block facedown. Fan out the seams at the center and fold them down. All 4 seams lie in different directions. If necessary, pick out a stitch or 2 at the center so the seams lie flat; then press the seams.

Sewing Nine-Patch Pinwheel Quilts

1. Place the 6 Pinwheel blocks in position.

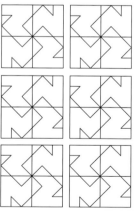

Position blocks.

2. Pick 2 blocks and place them right sides together. The center seams of the Pinwheel blocks lie in oppo-site directions and help to align the blocks.

3. Start at the center and sew one-half of the seam. Then start at the center again and sew the other half. Be careful each time to match critical seams. In pressing, I almost always treat these junctions like the center of a pinwheel (page 64), no matter how many seams are involved. One or 2 stitches are picked out before I fan out the seams.

You may choose to press all the seams to one side instead. In this case I suggest "asking" the seam which way it wants to go.

The key is to press identical seams in the same direction in all the blocks.

4. Repeat steps 2 and 3 to join 3 pairs of blocks. Press.

5. Join 2 block pairs together, starting at the center and stitching outward as in Step 3. Where 4 blocks meet, you need to pick out a stitch or 2 before you can fan out the seams and press them.

6. As before, join the remaining block pair to the piece created in Step 5. Press.

Binding

In this book, the binding is not included as part of the design process for the quilt tops. You will need to add extra yardage to finish your quilt to include batting, backing, and binding.

ORION

Orion, the quilt, is named after Orion, a town in southeast Alberta. In 1916 the town was named after Orion, the star constellation. The constellation, in turn, was named after Orion, the giant hunter of Greek mythology. Who the giant hunter was named after is anybody's guess. Possibly a rich uncle.

Orion, Wayne Kollinger, 2007, 24½" × 33½"

Fabric	Yardage*	Total Length of 2" Strips	Number of Cut Pieces	Size of Cut Pieces
Black 1	¼ yard or 6" × 40"	90"	12	2" × 3½"
			24	2" × 2"
Dark red 2	⅛ yard or 4" × 40"	42"	12	2" × 3½"
Red 3	⅛ yard or 4" × 40"	66"	12	2" × 3½"
			12	2" × 2"
Magenta 4	⅛ yard or 4" × 40"	42"	12	2" × 3½"
Light magenta 5	⅛ yard or 4" × 40"	66"	12	2" × 3½"
			12	2" × 2"
Dark purple 6	⅛ yard or 4" × 40"	42"	12	2" × 3½"
Purple 7	⅛ yard or 4" × 40"	42"	12	2" × 3 ½"
Light purple 8	⅛ yard or 4" × 40"	66"	12	2" × 3½"
			12	2" × 2"
White 9	¼ yard or 8" × 40" (blocks)	156"	24	2" × 3½"
			36	2" × 2"
	⅓ yard or 10½" × 40" (borders)	N/A	2	3½" × 18½" (D)
			2	3½" × 33½" (E)
	⅝ yard or 18½" × 40" (total)	Total white yardage for blocks and borders		

These are minimum quantities. I recommend that you increase the amounts by at least 25% to allow for squaring up the fabric, cutting errors, and waste.

Orion Nine-Patch Units

Make the vertical strip units by sewing pieces A1 and A2 together to make the A strip units; then pieces B1, B2, and B3 for the B strip units; and then pieces C1, C2, C3, and C4 for the C strip units. Be careful to place the colored pieces as shown. Next, sew the A, B, and C strip units together, making 12 of Unit F and 12 of Unit G. See Sewing Nine-Patch Pinwheel Units on page 64.

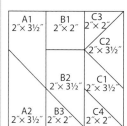

Basic *Orion* nine-patch unit; 4½" × 4½" finished

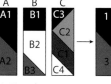

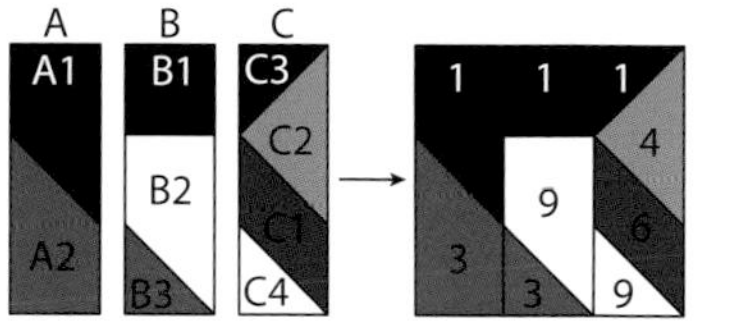

Unit F; make 12.

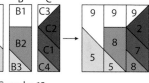

Unit G; make 12.

Orion Pinwheel Blocks

Assemble the 24 F and G nine-patch units into 6 Pinwheel blocks as shown. See Sewing Pinwheel Blocks on pages 64–65.

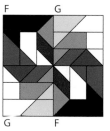

Pinwheel block; make 6.

Orion Quilt

1. Arrange the 6 Pinwheel blocks; then sew them together. See Sewing Nine-Patch Pinwheel Quilts on page 65.

2. Sew the D border pieces to the top and bottom. Press toward the borders. Then sew the E pieces to the sides. Press.

3. Add batting, backing, quilting, and binding and you're done.

Quilt construction

TEES

"Tees" is the kind of name a golfer might choose for a town—but not in this case. The town got its name for a more traditional reason. It was named after William E. Tees, the first owner of the property on which the town was built. I named this quilt after Tees for neither of these reasons. I did it just because.

Tees, Wayne Kollinger, 2008, 24½″ × 33½″

CUTTING

Fabric	Yardage*	Total Length of 2" Strips	Number of Cut Pieces	Size of Cut Pieces
Light burnt orange 1	¼ yard or 6" × 40"	108"	24	2" × 3½"
			12	2" × 2"
Burnt orange 2	¼ yard or 8" × 40"	150"	36	2" × 3½"
			12	2" × 2"
Light olive green 3	¼ yard or 6" × 40"	108"	24	2" × 3½"
			12	2" × 2"
Olive green 4	¼ yard or 8" × 40"	150"	36	2" × 3½"
			12	2" × 2"
Brown 5	¼ yard or 6" × 40" (blocks)	96"	48	2" × 2"
	⅓ yard or 10½" × 40" (borders)	N/A	2	3½" × 18½" (E)
			2	3½" × 33½" (F)
	⅝ yard or 16½" × 40" (total)	Total brown yardage for blocks and borders		
Black 6	¼ yard or 8" × 40"	144"	72	2" × 2"

*These are minimum quantities. I recommend that you increase the amounts by at least 25% to allow for squaring up the fabric, cutting errors, and waste.

Tees Nine-Patch Units

Make the vertical and horizontal strip units by sewing pieces A1 and A2 together to make the A strip units; then B1, B2, and B3 for the B strip units; then C1, C2, and C3 for the C strip units; and then D1, D2, D3, and D4 for the D strip units. Be careful to place the colored pieces as shown. Next, sew the A, B, C, and D strip units together into nine-patch units, making 12 of Unit G and 12 of Unit H. See Sewing Nine-Patch Pinwheel Units on page 64.

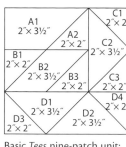

Basic Tees nine-patch unit;
4½" × 4½" finished

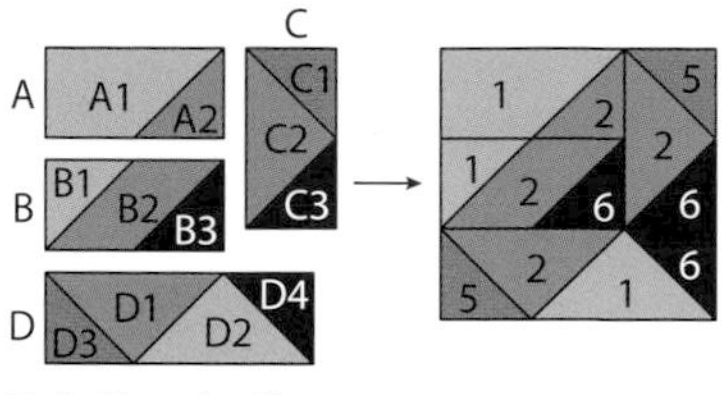

Unit G; make 12.

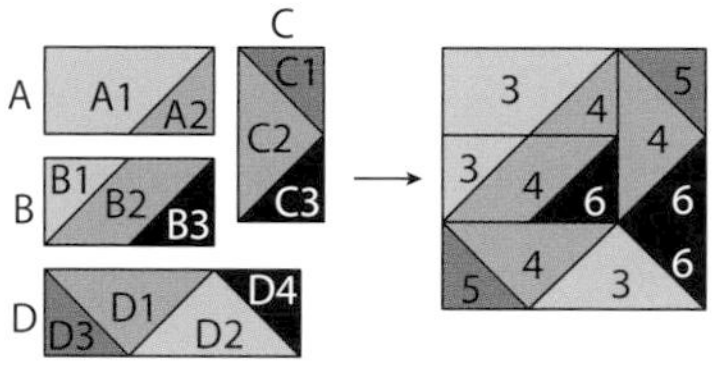

Unit H; make 12.

Tees Pinwheel Blocks

Assemble the 24 nine-patch units into 6 Pinwheel blocks as shown, making 3 of Block AA and 3 of Block BB. See Sewing Pinwheel Blocks on pages 64 65.

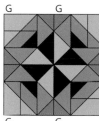
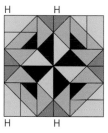

Block AA; make 3.

Block BB; make 3.

Tees Quilt

1. Arrange the 6 Pinwheel blocks; then sew them together. See Sewing Nine-Patch Pinwheel Quilts on page 65.

2. Sew the E border pieces to the top and bottom. Press toward the borders. Then sew the F pieces to the sides. Press.

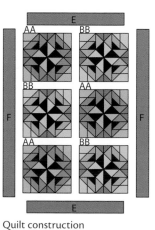

Quilt construction

3. Add batting, backing, quilting, and binding and you're done.

LAC DES ARCS

FINISHED QUILT SIZE: 24½″ × 33½″

Lac Des Arcs is a hamlet that takes its name from a nearby lake. I don't know how the lake got its name, but I do know that "lac des arcs" is French for both "lake of the bows" (as in "bow and arrow") and "lake of the arcs" (as in "arc of a circle"). Either version is fine with me for both the lake and this quilt.

Lac Des Arcs, Wayne Kollinger, 2007, 24½″ × 33½″

CUTTING

Fabric	Yardage*	Total Length of 2" Strips	Number of Cut Pieces	Size of Cut Pieces
Dark red 1	⅛ yard or 4" × 40"	42"	12	2" × 3½"
Red 2	⅓ yard or 10" × 40"	192"	12	2" × 5"
			24	2" × 3½"
			24	2" × 2"
Light red 3	⅛ yard or 4" × 40"	42"	12	2" × 3½"
Caramel 4	¼ yard or 6" × 40"	108"	12	2" × 5"
			24	2" × 2"
Light caramel 5	⅛ yard or 4" × 40"	42"	12	2" × 3½"
Pale caramel 6	⅛ yard or 4" × 40"	42"	12	2" × 3½"
Tan 7	⅓ yard or 12" × 40" (blocks)	234"	12	2" × 3½"
			96	2" × 2"
	⅓ yard or 10½" × 40" (borders)	N/A	2	3½" × 18½" (D)
			2	3½" × 33½" (E)
	⅝ yard or 22½" × 40" (total)		Total tan yardage for blocks and borders	
Darker tan 8	⅛ yard or 4" × 40"	42"	12	2" × 3½"

These are minimum quantities. I recommend that you increase the amounts by at least 25% to allow for squaring up the fabric, cutting errors, and waste.

Lac Des Arcs Nine-Patch Units

Make the vertical strip units by sewing pieces A1, A2, A3, and A4 together to make the A strip units, then B1, B2, and B3 for the B strip units, and then C1, C2, C3, and C4 for the C strip units. Be careful to place the colored pieces as shown. Next sew the A, B, and C strip units together into nine-patch units, making 12 of Unit F and 12 of Unit G. See Sewing Nine-Patch Pinwheel Units on page 64.

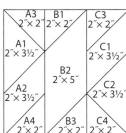

Basic Lac Des Arcs nine-patch unit; 4½" × 4½" finished

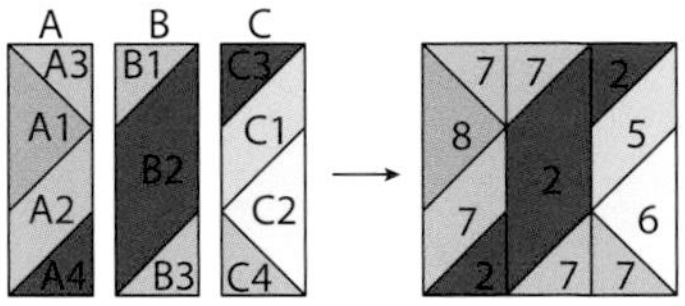

Unit F; make 12.

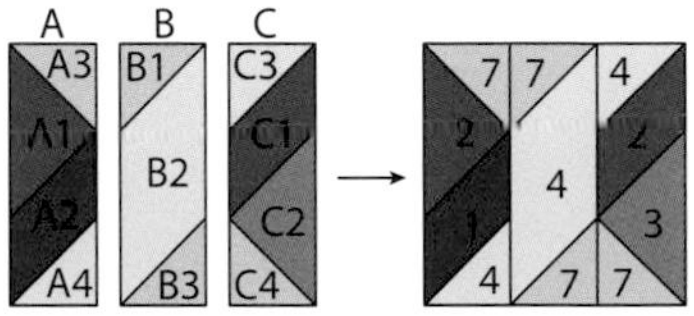

Unit G; make 12.

Lac Des Arcs Pinwheel Blocks

Assemble the 24 nine-patch units into 6 Pinwheel blocks as shown. See Sewing Pinwheel Blocks on pages 64–65.

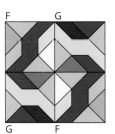

Pinwheel block; make 6.

Lac Des Arcs Quilt

1. Arrange the 6 Pinwheel blocks as shown; then sew them together. See Sewing Nine-Patch Pinwheel Quilts on page 65.

2. Sew the D border pieces to the top and bottom. Press toward the border. Then sew the E pieces to the sides. Press.

3. Add batting, backing, quilting, and binding and you're done.

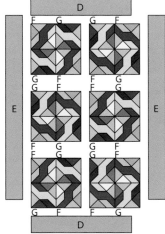

Quilt construction

MIRROR

FINISHED QUILT SIZE: 24½″ × 33½″

I named this quilt after the town of Mirror because I thought "Mirror" was an interesting name for a town and for a quilt. I later learned that the town was named after a newspaper, the *London Daily Mirror*, and that the streets in the town were named after the newspaper's staff. I wonder if they ever visited Mirror to see their streets.

Mirror, Wayne Kollinger, 2008, 24½″ × 33½″

CUTTING

Fabric	Yardage*	Total Length of 2" Strips	Number of Cut Pieces	Size of Cut Pieces
Deep brown 1	⅓ yard or 10½" × 40" (borders)	N/A	2	3½" × 18½" (E)
			2	3½" × 33½" (F)
Dark brindle 2	¼ yard or 6" × 40"	84"	24	2" × 3½"
Medium brindle 3	¼ yard or 6" × 40"	84"	24	2" × 3½"
Brindle 4	⅓ yard or 10" × 40"	168"	48	2" × 3½"
Light brindle 5	¼ yard or 6" × 40"	96"	48	2" × 2"
Dark green 6	¼ yard or 6" × 40"	84"	24	2" × 3½"
Green 7	⅛ yard or 4" × 40"	48"	24	2" × 2"

*These are minimum quantities. I recommend that you increase the amounts by at least 25% to allow for squaring up the fabric, cutting errors, and waste.

Mirror Nine-Patch Units

Make the vertical and horizontal strip units by sewing pieces A1 and A2 together to make the A strip units; then B1 and B2 for the B strip units; C1 and C2 for the C strip units; and then D1 and D2 for the D strip units. Be careful to place the colored pieces as shown. Next sew the A, B, C, and D strip units together to make 24 nine-patch units. See Sewing Nine-Patch Pinwheel Units on page 64.

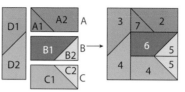

Basic *Mirror* nine-patch unit; 4½" × 4½" finished

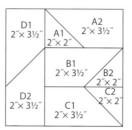

Make 24.

Mirror Pinwheel Blocks

Assemble the 24 nine-patch units into 6 Pinwheel blocks as shown. See Sewing Pinwheel Blocks on pages 64–65.

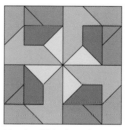

Pinwheel block; make 6.

Mirror Quilt

1. Arrange the 6 Pinwheel blocks as shown. Then sew them together. See Sewing Nine-Patch Pinwheel Quilts on page 65.

2. Sew the E border pieces to the top and bottom. Press toward the border. Then sew the F pieces to the sides. Press.

3. Add batting, backing, quilting, and binding and you're done.

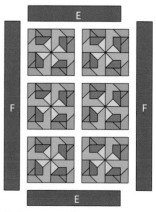

Quilt construction

TAWATINAW

FINISHED QUILT SIZE 27½″ × 36½″

When I finish designing a Nine-Patch Pinwheel quilt and it needs a name, I turn to my map of Alberta and look for a name that appeals to me. "Tawatinaw" appealed to me. It is the name of a village and of the river that runs through it. "Tawatinaw" derives from the Cree for "river that divides the hills."

Tawatinaw, Linda Hurd, 2009, 27½″ × 36½″

CUTTING

Fabric	Yardage*	Total Length of 2" Strips	Number of Cut Pieces	Size of Cut Pieces**
Dark purple 1	⅓ yard or 10" × 40"	181"	5	2" × 5"
			24	2" × 3½"
			36	2" × 2"
Light purple 2	⅓ yard or 10" × 40"	181"	5	2" × 5"
			24	2" × 3½"
			36	2" × 2"
White 3	¾ yard or 24" × 40"	478"	12	2" × 8"
			2	2" × 6½"
			48	2" × 5"
			6	2" × 3½"
			54	2" × 2"
Brown 4	⅛ yard or 4" × 40"	43"	2	2" × 8"
			4	2" × 5"
			2	2" × 3½"
Medium brown 5	⅛ yard or 4" × 40"	46"	2	2" × 8"
			6	2" × 5"
Dark brown 6	⅛ yard or 2" × 40"	40"	8	2" × 5"
Deep brown 7	⅛ yard or 4" × 40"	49"	2	2" × 8"
			2	2" × 6½"
			4	2" × 5"

*These are minimum quantities. I recommend that you increase the amounts by at least 25% to allow for squaring up the fabric, cutting errors, and waste.

**Includes pieces for Nine-Patch Pinwheel blocks and borders.

Tawatinaw Nine-Patch Units

Make vertical strip units by sewing pieces A1, A2, and A3 together to make the A strip units; B1 and B2 together for the B strip units; and then C1, C2, and C3 for the C strip units. Be careful to place the colored pieces as shown. Next sew the A, B, and C strip units together to make 12 L nine-patch units and 12 M nine-patch units. See Sewing Nine-Patch Pinwheel Units on page 64.

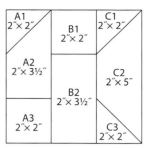

Basic *Tawatinaw* nine-patch unit; 4½" × 4½" finished

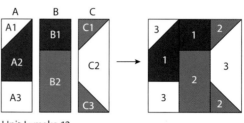

Unit L; make 12.

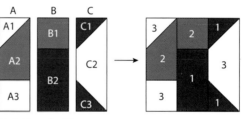

Unit M; make 12.

Tawatinaw Pinwheel Blocks

Assemble the 24 nine-patch units into 6 Pinwheel blocks as shown. See Sewing Pinwheel Blocks on pages 64–65.

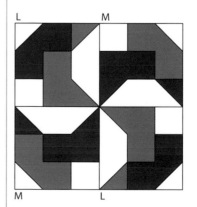

Pinwheel block; make 6.

Tawatinaw Quilt Top

Arrange the 6 Pinwheel blocks as shown. Then sew them together. See Sewing Nine-Patch Pinwheel Quilts on page 65.

Quilt construction

Tawatinaw Quilt Border

The border consists of 3 borders:

- Inner border: D, E, F, and G border units (added first)

- Middle border: H and I border units (2 of each; added second)

- Outer border: J and K border units (2 of each; added third)

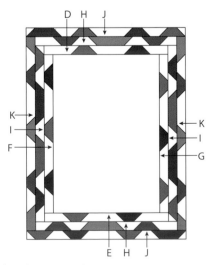

Border construction

In each case, add the side borders to the quilt top, then the top and bottom borders—starting with the inner border units, then adding the middle border units, and then the outer border units. Press as you go along. It is easiest to press toward the outer border.

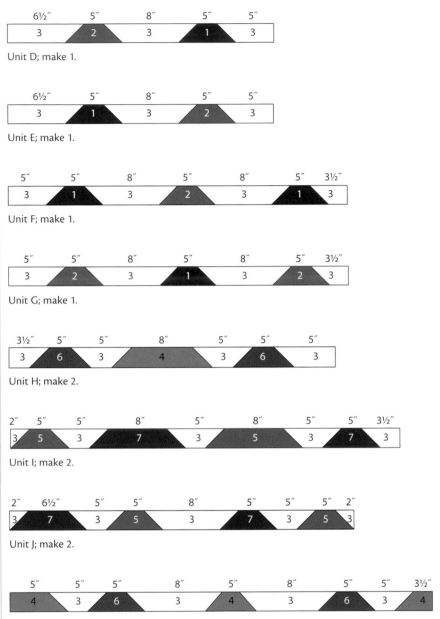

Unit D; make 1.

Unit E; make 1.

Unit F; make 1.

Unit G; make 1.

Unit H; make 2.

Unit I; make 2.

Unit J; make 2.

Unit K; make 2.

After the quilt top and the border are assembled, all that remains is to add batting, backing, quilting, and binding and you're done.

DUCHESS

When George V was King of England, his uncle Prince Arthur was Canada's 10th Governor General. The prince, one of Queen Victoria's nine children, was married to a Prussian princess, Duchess Luise Margarete. So the Canadian Pacific Railway decided to name a town in southeast Alberta "Duchess" in her honor. Not that any of this gossip matters; what matters is that I named this quilt after the town.

Duchess, Wayne Kollinger, 2008, 24½" × 33½"

CUTTING

Fabric	Yardage*	Total Length of 2" Strips	Number of Cut Pieces	Size of Cut Pieces
Yellow-green 1	¼ yard or 8" × 40"	121"	22	2" × 3½"
			22	2" × 2"
Light green 2	¼ yard or 6" × 40"	112"	8	2" × 5"
			16	2" × 3½"
			8	2" × 2"
Medium green 3	⅛ yard or 4" × 40"	77"	14	2" × 3½"
			14	2" × 2"
Dark green 4	⅓ yard or 10" × 40"	168"	12	2" × 5"
			24	2" × 3½"
			12	2" × 2"
White 5	¼ yard or 8" × 40" (blocks)	122"	4	2" × 5"
			20	2" × 3½"
			16	2" × 2"
	⅓ yard or 10½" × 40" (borders)	N/A	2	3½" × 18½" (E)
			2	3½" × 33½" (F)
	⅝ yard or 18½" × 40" (total)	Total white yardage for blocks and borders.		

These are minimum quantities. I recommend that you increase the amounts by at least 25% to allow for squaring up the fabric, cutting errors, and waste.

Duchess Nine-Patch Units

To assemble the *Duchess* nine-patch units, first make the horizontal strip units by sewing pieces A1 and A2 together to make the A strip units; B1 and B2 for the B strip units; and then C1, C2, C3, and C4 for the C strip units. Next sew the A, B, and C strip units together to make the nine-patch units as shown. See Sewing Nine-Patch Pinwheel Units on page 64.

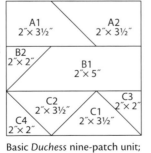

Basic *Duchess* nine-patch unit; 4½" × 4½" finished

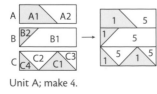

Unit A; make 4. 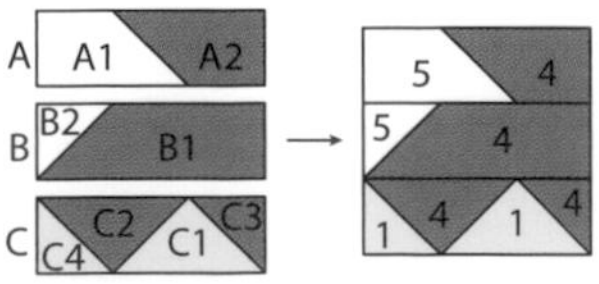　　　Unit B; make 6.

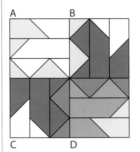

Unit C; make 6.

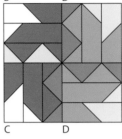

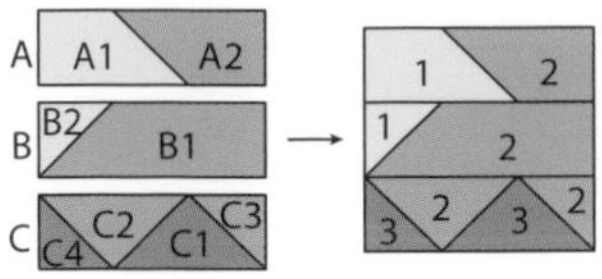

Unit D; make 8.

Duchess Pinwheel Blocks

Assemble the 24 nine-patch units into 6 Pinwheel blocks, making 4 of Block AA and 2 of Block BB as shown. See Sewing Pinwheel Blocks on pages 64–65.

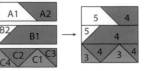

Block AA; make 4.　　　Block BB; make 2.

Duchess Quilt

1. Arrange the 6 Pinwheel blocks as shown. Then sew them together. See Sewing Nine-Patch Pinwheel Quilts on page 65.

2. Sew the E border pieces to the top and bottom. Press toward the border. Then sew the F pieces to the sides. Press.

3. Add batting, backing, quilting, and binding and you're done.

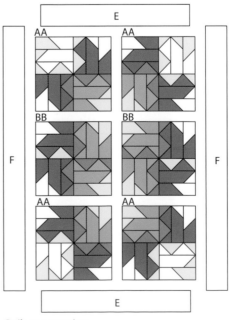

Quilt construction

ABOUT THE AUTHOR

photo by: Julia Price

Where do quilt designers come from? Wayne Kollinger began as a critic. He would go with his wife to quilt shows, where he would occasionally see pieced lettering. Some of it wasn't very good, and he said so. After a while his wife, Linda, challenged him: "If you think you can do better, go ahead."

So he learned to sew and to quilt. Before long, he had designed several dozen different pieced alphabets. That led to designing quilts, teaching quilt classes, doing trunk shows, and selling his quilt patterns. Now he has written a book on quilt design that is based on asking three simple questions: "What if...?" "Do I like it? and "Why?"

Where do quilt designers come from? They come from everywhere and anywhere. Wayne wrote this book to show how easy it can be for you to design your own quilts.

Great Titles *from* C&T PUBLISHING